VOGUE® KNITTING
Very Easy Sweaters

VOGUE® KNITTING
Very Easy Sweaters
50 simple, stylish designs

THE EDITORS OF VOGUE® KNITTING MAGAZINE

sixth&springbooks
NEW YORK

sixth&spring books

161 Avenue of the Americas, New York, NY 10013

Editorial Director	Vice President
JOY AQUILINO	TRISHA MALCOLM
Developmental Editor	Publisher
LISA SILVERMAN	CARRIE KILMER
Art Director	Production Manager
DIANE LAMPHRON	DAVID JOINNIDES
Yarn Editor	President
CHRISTINA BEHNKE	ART JOINNIDES
Layout and Design	Chairman
JOY MAKON	JAY STEIN
Editorial Assistant	
JOHANNA LEVY	

PHOTO CREDITS

All photography by Rose Callahan, except as noted below:

Paul Amato for LVARepresents.com: pages 2, 20, 34, 36, 46, 49, 50, 57-58, 64, 76, 78-80, 82-84, 99-100, 105-106, 108, 114, 117, 134, 136-138, 170, 173, 180, 183-184, 187

Haitem: pages 53-54

Library of Congress Cataloging-in-Publication Data is available from the Library of Congress.

ISBN: 978-1-936096-66-4

MANUFACTURED IN CHINA

1 3 5 7 9 10 8 6 4 2

First Edition

Contents

Chic
Knitwear
Made *Easy*

For more than thirty years it's been our mission at *Vogue Knitting* to bring knitters the very best in knitwear design. While one of our primary goals is to inspire knitters at all skill levels to challenge themselves to become more technically accomplished, it isn't hard to understand why Very Easy patterns—which feature basic stitches and simple finishing—are among our most popular, both in print and online.

Very Easy designs make creating fabulous handknit garments accessible to every knitter. They're ideal for beginners who are ready to knit their first sweaters, as well as for more proficient knitters with busy schedules who are looking to make the most of their limited knitting time. This collection of fifty fabulous Very Easy sweaters proves beyond the shadow of a doubt that knitwear design doesn't have to be complicated or time-consuming to be chic, wearable, and timeless.

With so many amazing garments to choose from, the main challenge was to limit the collection to only fifty. The process of choosing the designs was a pleasure for me and my editors, who thoroughly enjoyed poring over the pages of the magazine's recent issues to revisit these stunners. It was also wonderful to reconsider the work of some of our regular (and most celebrated) contributors, including Cathy Carron, Rosemary Drysdale, Louisa Harding, Shiri Mor, Mari Lynn Patrick, Norah Gaughan, Josh Bennett, Yoko Hatta, and John Brinegar. Their thoughtful experimentation with the basic elements of our craft—simple stitch patterns, garment shape, colorwork, and fiber—has yielded undeniably exciting pieces that are destined to become classics.

Trisha Malcolm
Editorial Director, *Vogue Knitting*

STOCKINETTE

LIGHT & EASY

DRAMATIC SHAPES

CABLES

STRIPES & COLORWORK

Drape Front Sweater

Layering is a piece of cake with Roberta Rosenfield's twisted pullover. The stockinette fabric, stitched side to side, is twisted before grafting to form the luxurious drape front.

SIZES
Sized for Small, Medium/Large, 1X and shown in size Small.

KNITTED MEASUREMENTS
Bust 44 (48, 52)"/112 (122, 132)cm
Length 18½ (19¾, 20¼)"/47 (50, 51.5)cm
Upper arm 16 (17, 17½)"/40.5 (43, 44.5)cm

MATERIALS
• 5 (5, 6) 3½oz/100g hanks (each approx 220yd/200m) of AslanTrends *Royal Alpaca* (alpaca) in #402 andean coal (4)

• One pair size 8 (5mm) needles OR SIZE TO OBTAIN GAUGE

• Stitch markers

GAUGE
20 sts and 26 rows = 4"/10cm over St st using size 8 (5mm) needles.
TAKE TIME TO CHECK GAUGE.

NOTE
Front and back of sweater are worked in St st. In finishing, front of sweater is twisted once so that ½ of the drape front is St st and ½ is reverse St st (see photo). Because back width is determined lengthwise by counting rows, use a thin cotton thread pulled through the fabric every 6 to 8" (15 to 20.5cm) for easier counting and remove thread in the finishing.

BACK AND ½ LEFT SLEEVE
Beg at the left sleeve cuff edge, cast on 40 (42, 44) sts. Work in St st for 8 (8¼, 8¼)"/20.5 (21, 21)cm. Place a marker at beg of the last WS row (this is the shoulder edge).

Back side seam
Next row (RS) Cast on 52 (56, 58) sts—92 (98, 102) sts. Then, work in St st until piece measures 8½ (9½, 10½)"/21.5 (24, 26.5)cm from the marker.
Next row (RS) K to last 6 sts, weave a contrast thread through these sts (to mark center back neck), k rem 6 sts. Then cont in St st until piece measures 8½ (9½, 10½)"/21.5 (24, 26.5)cm from the center marked back neck.

Back and ½ right sleeve
Next row (RS) Bind off 52 (56, 58) sts, knit to end— 40 (42, 44) sts. Work in St st for 8 (8¼, 8¼)"/20.5 (21, 21)cm from the side seam. Bind off sts loosely.

FRONT AND ½ RIGHT SLEEVE
Beg at the right sleeve cuff edge, cast on 40 (42, 44) sts. Work in St st for 8 (8¼, 8¼)"/20.5 (21, 21)cm. Place a marker at beg of the last WS row (this is the shoulder edge).

Front side seam

Next row (RS) Cast on 52 (56, 58) sts—92 (98, 102) sts. Then work in St st until piece measures 34 (38, 42)"/86.5 (96.5, 106.5)cm from the side seam marker, end with a RS row.

Front and ½ left sleeve

Next row (WS) Bind off 52 (56, 58) sts, purl to end— 40 (42, 44) sts. Work in St st for 8 (8¼, 8¼)"/20.5 (21, 21)cm from side seam. Bind off loosely.

FINISHING

Block pieces to measurements. Place a safety pin or removable marker at 4"/10cm each side of the center back neck. This will mark the 8"/20cm-wide back neck opening.

Using mattress st from the RS, sew the right top of sleeve seam of the front and back tog. Sew the right body seam edge in same way. Lay the partially finished sweater on a flat surface and twist the left side of the front and ½ left sleeve with one counter-clockwise twist so that the reverse or purl side of the fabric lines up with the left side of the garment. From this position, sew the left front side seam and top of sleeve in place in same way as previous side. After trying on sweater, adjust the width of the back neck, if desired, by taking in more fabric at the neck seam. ■

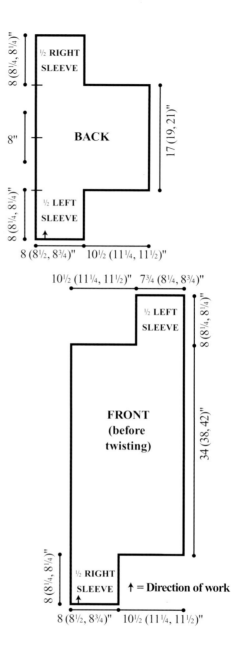

Buttoned Cardi

Shapely and chic, Louisa Harding's cardi is full of smart touches, including cuffs vented with a button detail and skinny seed-stitch edges and collar.

SIZES
Sized for X-Small, Small, Medium, Large, 1X, 2X, 3X and shown in size X-Small.

KNITTED MEASUREMENTS
Bust (closed) 32 (35, 38, 42, 46, 50, 54)"/81 (89, 96.5, 106.5, 117, 127, 137)cm
Length 20¼ (20¾, 21¾, 22¼, 23¼, 23¾, 24¾)"/51.5 (52.5, 55, 56.5, 59, 60.5, 63)cm
Upper arm 12 (13, 14, 15, 16, 17, 18)"/30.5 (33, 35.5, 38, 40.5, 43, 45.5)cm

MATERIALS
• 8 (9, 10, 11, 13, 14, 16) 1¾oz/50g balls (each approx 110yd/100m) of Louisa Harding/KFI *Grace Wool & Silk* (wool/silk) in #11 royal (MC) ③

• 2 (2, 3, 3, 3, 3, 4) balls in #6 ruby (CC)

• One pair each sizes 3 and 5 (3.25 and 3.75mm) needles OR SIZE TO OBTAIN GAUGE

• Stitch holder and stitch markers

• Three ¹¹⁄₁₆"/17mm buttons; six ½"/13mm buttons

GAUGE
24 sts and 30 rows = 4"/10cm over St st using larger needles.
TAKE TIME TO CHECK GAUGE.

SEED STITCH
Row 1 (RS) *K1, p1; rep from * to end.
Row 2 K the purl sts and p the knit sts.
Rep row 2 for seed st.

BACK
With smaller needles and CC, cast on 86 (96, 104, 116, 128, 140, 152) sts. Work in seed st for 4 (4, 4, 4, 6, 6, 6) rows. Change to larger needles and MC. Cont in St st and work even for 1"/2.5cm, end with a WS row.

Side shaping
Inc row (RS) K3, M1, knit to last 3 sts, M1, k3. Rep

inc row every 16th (16th, 16th, 16th, 18th, 18th, 18th) row 4 times more—96 (106, 114, 126, 138, 150, 162) sts. Work even until piece measures 12 (12, 12½, 12½, 13, 13, 13½)"/30.5 (30.5, 31.5, 31.5, 33, 33, 34)cm from beg, end with a WS row.

Armhole shaping

Bind off 4 (5, 5, 7, 8, 9, 10) sts at beg of next 2 rows, then 3 (3, 3, 3, 4, 4, 5) sts at beg of next 2 rows—82 (90, 98, 106, 114, 124, 132) sts.
Dec row (RS) K3, k2tog, knit to last 5 sts, ssk, k3. Purl next row. Rep last 2 rows 2 (3, 4, 5, 6, 8, 9) times more—76 (82, 88, 94, 100, 106, 112) sts. Work even until armhole measures 7½ (8, 8½, 9, 9½, 10, 10½)"/17.5 (19, 20.5, 21.5, 23, 25.5, 26.5)cm, end with a WS row.
Mark center 30 (30, 34, 34, 38, 38, 40) sts.

Shoulder and neck shaping

Bind off 7 (8, 8, 9, 9, 10, 11) sts at beg of next 4 rows, then 6 (7, 8, 9, 10, 11, 11) sts at beg of next 2 rows, AT SAME TIME, bind off center 30 (30, 34, 34, 38, 38, 40) sts. Working both sides at once, bind off 3 sts from each neck edge once.

LEFT FRONT

With smaller needles and CC, cast on 42 (48, 52, 58, 64, 70, 76) sts. Work in seed st for 4 (4, 4, 4, 6, 6, 6) rows. Change to larger needles and MC. Cont in St st and work even for 1"/2.5cm, end with a WS row.

Side shaping

Inc row (RS) K3, M1, knit to end. Rep inc row every 16th (16th, 16th, 16th, 18th, 18th, 18th) row 4 times more—47 (53, 57, 63, 69, 75, 81) sts. Work

even until piece measures same length as back to underarm, end with a WS row.

Armhole shaping

At armhole edge, bind off 4 (5, 5, 7, 8, 9, 10) sts once, then 3 (3, 3, 3, 4, 4, 5) sts once, end with a WS row—40 (45, 49, 53, 57, 62, 66) sts.
Dec row (RS) K3, k2tog, knit to end. Purl next row. Rep last 2 rows 2 (3, 4, 5, 6, 8, 9) times more—37 (41, 44, 47, 50, 53, 56) sts. Work even until armhole measures 5½ (6, 6½, 7, 7½, 8, 8½)"/14 (15, 16.5, 17.5, 19, 20.5, 21.5)cm, end with a RS row.

Neck shaping

At neck edge, bind off 10 (11, 13, 13, 15, 15, 16) sts once, then 4 sts once, end with a WS row. Dec 1 st from neck edge on next row, then every other row twice more—20 (23, 24, 27, 28, 31, 33) sts. Work even until piece measures same length as back to shoulder, end with a WS row.

Shoulder shaping

At armhole edge, bind off 7 (8, 8, 9, 9, 10, 11) sts twice, then 6 (7, 8, 9, 10, 11, 11) sts once.

RIGHT FRONT

With smaller needles and CC, cast on 42 (48, 52, 58, 64, 70, 76) sts. Work as for left front, end with a WS row.

Side shaping

Inc row (RS) Knit to last 3 sts, M1, k3. Rep inc row every 16th (16th, 16th, 16th, 18th, 18th, 18th) row 4 times more—47 (53, 57, 63, 69, 75, 81) sts. Work even until piece measures same length as back to underarm, end with a RS row.

Armhole shaping

At armhole edge, bind off 4 (5, 5, 7, 8, 9, 10) sts once, then 3 (3, 3, 3, 4, 4, 5) sts once, end with a WS row—40 (45, 49, 53, 57, 62, 66) sts.

Dec row (RS) Knit to last 5 sts, ssk, k3. Purl next row. Rep last 2 rows 2 (3, 4, 5, 6, 8, 9) times more—37 (41, 44, 47, 50, 53, 56) sts. Work even until armhole measures 5½ (6, 6½, 7, 7½, 8, 8½)"/14 (15, 16.5, 17.5, 19, 20.5, 21.5)cm, end with a WS row.

Neck shaping

At neck edge, bind off 10 (11, 13, 13, 15, 15, 16) sts once, then 4 sts once, end with a WS row. Dec 1 st from neck edge on next row, then every other row twice more—20 (23, 24, 27, 28, 31, 33) sts. Work even until piece measures same length as back to shoulder, end with a RS row.

Shoulder shaping

At armhole edge, bind off 7 (8, 8, 9, 9, 10, 11) sts twice, then 6 (7, 8, 9, 10, 11, 11) sts once.

LEFT SLEEVE

NOTE Cuff is made in two sections.

For RH section, work as foll: with smaller needles and CC, cast on 40 (40, 40, 44, 44, 46, 46) sts. Work in seed st for 16 rows. Break yarn. Place sts on holder. For LH section, work as foll: with smaller needles and CC, cast on 20 (20, 20, 24, 24, 26, 26) sts. Work in seed st for 16 rows.

Cuff joining

NEXT ROW (RS) Work in seed st over 20 (20, 20, 24, 24, 26, 26) sts, work in seed st across 40 (40, 40, 44, 44, 46, 46) sts on holder—60 (60, 60, 68, 68, 72, 72) sts. Cont in seed st for 3 rows more.

Change to larger needles and MC. Cont in St st and work even for 1"/2.5cm, end with a WS row.

Inc row (RS) K3, M1, knit to last 3 sts, M1, k3. Rep inc row every 4th row 0 (0, 0, 0, 0, 1, 8) times more, every 6th row 0 (0, 5, 1, 11, 13, 9) times, every 8th row 0 (3, 6, 9, 2, 0, 0) times, every 10th row 0 (5, 0, 0, 0, 0, 0) times, every 14th row 5 (0, 0, 0, 0, 0, 0) times—72 (78, 84, 90, 96, 102, 108) sts. Work even until piece measures 14 (14, 14½, 14½, 15, 15, 15½)"/35.5 (35.5, 37, 37, 38, 38, 39.5)cm from beg, end with a WS row.

Cap shaping

Bind off 4 (5, 5, 7, 8, 9, 10) sts at beg of next 2 rows, then 3 (3, 3, 3, 4, 4, 5) sts at beg of next 2 rows. Dec 1 st each side on next row, then every other row 4 (5, 6, 7, 8, 9, 10) times more, end with a WS row. Dec 1 st each side on next row, then every 4th row 5 times more, end with a RS row. Purl 1 row, knit 1 row. Dec 1 st each side on next 3 rows. Bind off 4 sts at beg of next 4 rows. Bind off rem 14 (16, 20, 20, 20, 22, 22) sts.

RIGHT SLEEVE

Cuff

For RH section, work as foll: with smaller needles and CC, cast on 20 (20, 20, 24, 24, 26, 26) sts. Work in seed st for 16 rows. Break yarn. Place sts on holder. For LH section, work as foll: with smaller needles and CC, cast on 40 (40, 40, 44, 44, 46, 46) sts. Work in seed st for 16 rows.

Cuff joining

Next row (RS) Work in seed st over 40 (40, 40, 44, 44, 46, 46) sts, then work in seed st across 20 (20, 20, 24, 24, 26, 26) sts on holder—60 (60, 60, 68,

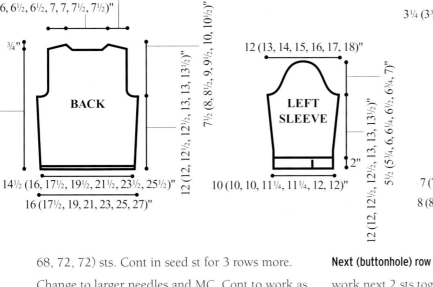

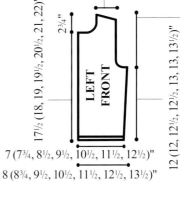

68, 72, 72) sts. Cont in seed st for 3 rows more. Change to larger needles and MC. Cont to work as for left sleeve.

FINISHING

Lightly block pieces to measurements. Sew shoulder seams.

Button band

With RS facing, smaller needles and CC, pick up and k 96 (100, 104, 108, 112, 116, 122) sts evenly spaced along left front edge. Work in seed st for 3 (3, 3, 3, 5, 5, 5) rows. Bind off in seed st. Place markers for 6 buttons along right front edge, with the first ½"/1.3cm from lower edge, the last 2½ (2½, 2¾, 2¾, 3¼, 3¼, 3½)"/6.5 (6.5, 7, 7, 8, 8, 9)cm below neck edge, and the others evenly spaced between.

Buttonhole band

With RS facing, smaller needles and CC, pick up and k 96 (100, 104, 108, 112, 116, 122) sts evenly spaced along right front edge. Work in seed st for 1 (1, 1, 1, 3, 3, 3) rows.

Next (buttonhole) row (RS) *Work in seed st to marker, work next 2 sts tog, yo; rep from * 5 times more, work to end. Cont in seed st for 2 rows more. Bind off in seed st.

Neckband and collar

With RS facing, smaller needles and CC, pick up and k 26 (26, 28, 28, 32, 32, 34) sts evenly spaced along right neck edge to shoulder seam, 36 (36, 40, 40, 44, 44, 46) sts along back neck edge to next shoulder seam, 26 (26, 28, 28, 32, 32, 34) sts along left front neck edge—88 (88, 96, 96, 108, 108, 114) sts. Work in seed st for 1 row.

Next (buttonhole) row (RS) K1, p2tog, yo, work to end. Cont in seed st for 2 rows more. Bind off 4 sts at beg of next 2 rows—80 (80, 88, 88, 100, 100, 106) sts. Cont in seed st for 2½ (2½, 2½, 3, 3, 3½, 3½)"/6.5 (6.5, 6.5, 7.5, 7.5, 9, 9)cm. Bind off loosely in seed st. Set in sleeves. Sew side and sleeve seams. Sew a large button to each cuff, just above split. Sew last large button opposite top buttonhole. Sew on small buttons opposite 6 rem buttonholes. ■

Garter Yoke Cardi

Seamless both literally and figuratively, Melissa LaBarre's garter-yoke cardigan is worked up top with short rows that morph into raglan shaping and stockinette stitch just before you separate for the sleeves.

SIZES

Sized for Small, Medium, Large, X-Large and shown in size Small.

KNITTED MEASUREMENTS

Bust (closed) 34 (36, 38, 40)"/86 (91.5, 96.5, 101.5)cm
Length 21 (21½, 22½, 23½)"/53 (54.5, 57, 59.5)cm
Upper arm 11 (12, 13½, 14¼)"/28 (30.5, 34, 37)cm

MATERIALS

• 9 (10, 11, 12) 1¾oz/50g hanks (each approx 102yd/93m) of Plymouth Yarn Co. *Royal Llama Silk* (llama/silk) in #1845 cranberry ④

• One size 7 (4.5mm) circular needle, 40"/100cm long, OR SIZE TO OBTAIN GAUGE

• One set (5) size 7 (4.5mm) double-pointed needles (dpn)

• Scrap yarn

• 9 (9, 10, 10) ⅝"/15mm buttons

• Stitch markers

GAUGE

18 sts and 28 rows = 4"/10cm over St st using size 7 (4.5mm) needles.
TAKE TIME TO CHECK GAUGE.

SHORT ROW WRAP & TURN (w&t)

Instructions given for RS row; WS row in parentheses.
1) Wyib (wyif), sl next st purlwise.
2) Move yarn between the needles to the front (back).
3) Sl the same st back to LH needle. Turn work. One st is wrapped.
When working the wrapped st, insert RH needle under the wrap and work it tog with the corresponding st on needle.

YOKE

Beg at the neck edge, with circular needle, cast on 113 sts. Do not join, work back and forth in rows. Knit 4 rows.
Buttonhole row 5 (RS) K to last 3 sts, yo, k2tog, k1.
Row 6 Knit.

Shape with short rows

*Short row 7 (RS) K78, w&t.
Next row (WS) K43, w&t. Knit to end of row (do not pick up wraps)*.

Row 8 (WS) Knit all sts, picking up wraps.

Row 9 Rep short row 7 from * to *.

Row 10 Rep row 8.

Rows 11–14 Knit.

Inc row 15 K5, *k2, k1 into front of back of next st (for inc 1 st); rep from * to last 6 sts, k6—147 sts.

Rows 16–20 Knit.

Row 21 Rep buttonhole row 5.

Rows 22–28 Knit.

Inc row 29 K5, *k3, inc 1 st in next st; rep from * to last 6 sts, k6—181 sts.

Rows 30–36 Knit.

Row 37 Rep buttonhole row 5.

Rows 38–40 Knit.

Shape the raglan

Cont to work the first 5 sts and last 5 sts of body in garter st, for front bands, AND work buttonhole row every 16th row as established, work the rem of the cardigan in St st with raglan shaping as foll:

Inc row 1 (RS) K31, inc 1 st in next st (left front), pm; inc 1 st in next st, k28, inc 1 st in next st (sleeve), pm, inc 1 st in next st, k55, inc 1 st in next st (back), pm; inc 1 st in next st, k28, inc 1 st in next st (sleeve), pm; inc 1 st in next st, k31 (right front)—8 sts inc'd.

Row 2 K5, purl to last 5 sts, k5.

Inc row 3 (RS) *K to 1 st before marker, inc 1 st in next st, sl marker, inc 1 st in next st; rep from * 3 times more, k to end.

Row 4 K5, purl to last 5 sts, k5.

Rep rows 3 and 4 for 8 (10, 13, 15) times more—261 (277, 301, 317) sts.

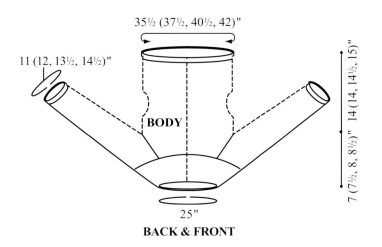

35½ (37½, 40½, 42)"

11 (12, 13½, 14½)"

BODY

7 (7½, 8, 8½)" 14 (14, 14½, 15)"

25"
BACK & FRONT

Divide for the body

Next row (RS) K to the first marker, remove marker, sl the sts up to the 2nd marker to scrap yarn for first sleeve, sl marker to needle (for side seam), k across back sts to next marker, remove marker, sl the sts up to the 4th marker to scrap yarn for 2nd sleeve, sl marker to needle (for side seam), k to end.

There are 161 (169, 181, 189) sts for body and 50 (54, 60, 64) sts for each sleeve. Cont to work the body sts only in St st with 5-st garter bands (and buttonholes) for 3"/7.5cm.

Waist shaping

Dec row (RS) *K to 4 sts before marker, ssk, k2, sl marker, k2, k2tog; rep from * once, k to end. Rep dec row every 4th row 3 times more—145 (153, 165, 173) sts. Work even for 2"/5cm from last dec row.

Inc row (RS) *K to 3 sts before marker, M1, k3, sl marker, k3, M1; rep from * once, k to end. Rep inc row every 4th row 3 times more—161 (169, 181, 189) sts. Work even until piece measures 13 (13, 13½, 14)"/33 (33, 34, 35.5)cm measured along the side seam. Knit 8 rows. Bind off.

SLEEVES

Place the sts of one sleeve on dpn, evenly divided over 4 needles. Join and work in rnds of St st for 15½"/39.5cm. Then, [p 1 rnd, k 1 rnd] 4 times for garter st border. Bind off. Work 2nd sleeve in same way.

FINISHING

Sew on buttons. ■

Sleeveless Cardi

Faith Hale's dolman cardi has a simple stockinette body and wide seed-stitch front bands and collar.

SIZES

Sized for Small, Medium, Large, 1X, 2X and shown in size Small.

KNITTED MEASUREMENTS

Lower edge (closed) 33½ (37½, 41½, 45½, 49½)"/85 (95, 105.5, 115.4, 125.5)cm

Bust (closed) 46 (50, 54, 58, 62)"/117 (127, 137, 147, 157.5)cm

Length 22½ (23, 24, 25, 25½)"/57 (58.5, 61, 63, 64.5)cm

MATERIALS

• 7 (8, 9, 10, 11) 1¾oz/50g hanks (each approx 138yd/126m) of Alchemy Yarns of Transformation *Silk Purse* (silk) in #76e topaz 🔳

• One pair size 5 (3.75mm) needles OR SIZE TO OBTAIN GAUGE

• Size 5 (3.75mm) circular needle, 32"/80cm long

GAUGE

24 sts and 30 rows = 4"/10cm over St st using size 5 (3.75mm) needles.
TAKE TIME TO CHECK GAUGE.

SEED STITCH

(over an even number of sts)

Row 1 (RS) *K1, p1; rep from * to end.

Row 2 K the purl sts and p the knit sts.

Rep row 2 for seed st.

K1, P1 RIB

(over an even number of sts)

Row 1 *K1, p1; rep from * to end.

Row 2 K the knit sts and p the purl sts.

Rep row 2 for k1, p1 rib.

BACK

With straight needles, cast on 93 (105, 115, 127, 137) sts. Work in seed st for 1½"/4cm. K next row on RS, inc 8 (8, 10, 10, 12) sts evenly spaced across—101 (113, 125, 137, 149) sts. P 1 row. Cont in St st (k on RS, p on WS), inc 1 st each side every 8th row 5 times, every 4th row twice, every other row 13 times—141 (153, 165, 177, 189) sts. Work even until piece measures 12 (12, 12, 12½, 12½)"/30.5 (30.5, 30.5, 31.5, 31.5)cm from beg.

Armhole shaping

Bind off 2 sts at beg of next 12 rows—117 (129, 141, 153, 165) sts. Work even for 3 (3½, 4, 4½, 5)"/7.5 (9, 10, 11.5, 12.5)cm.
Cast on 2 sts at beg of next 12 rows—141 (153, 165, 177, 189) sts. Work even until armhole measures 6½ (7, 8, 8½, 9)"/16.5 (18, 20.5, 21.5, 23)cm.

Shoulder shaping

Bind off 3 (3, 3, 3, 5) sts at beg of next 24 (24, 14, 6, 6) rows, 2 (4, 4, 4, 4) sts at beg of next 6 (6, 16, 24, 24) rows. Bind off rem 57 (57, 59, 63, 63) sts for back neck.

LEFT FRONT

With straight needles, cast on 33 (39, 44, 50, 55) sts. Work in seed st for 1½"/4cm. K next row on RS, inc 2 (2, 3, 3, 4) sts evenly spaced across—35 (41 47, 53, 59) sts. P 1 row. Cont in St st, inc 1 st at side (beg of RS rows) same as back—55 (61, 67, 73, 79) sts.

Armhole shaping

Bind off 2 sts at beg of next 6 RS rows—43 (49, 55, 61, 67) sts. Work even for 3 (3½, 4, 4½, 5)"/7.5 (9, 10, 11.5, 12.5)cm.

Cast on 2 sts at beg of next 6 RS rows—49 (55 (61, 67, 73, 79) sts. Work even until armhole measures 6½ (7, 8, 8½, 9)"/16.5 (18, 20.5, 21.5, 23)cm.

Shoulder shaping

Bind off 3 (3, 3, 3, 5) sts at beg of next 12 (12, 7, 3, 3) RS rows, 2 (4, 4, 4, 4) sts at beg of next 3 (3, 8, 12, 12) RS rows. Bind off rem 13 (13, 14, 16, 16) sts.

RIGHT FRONT

Work to correspond to left front, working all shaping at beg of WS rows.

FINISHING

Block pieces to measurements. Sew shoulder seams, sew last 13 (13, 14, 16, 16) sts on each front along back neck.

Front bands and collar

With RS facing and circular needle, beg at lower right front edge, pick up and k 118 (120, 126, 132, 134) sts evenly along right front edge, 33 sts along back neck and 118 (120, 126, 132, 134) sts

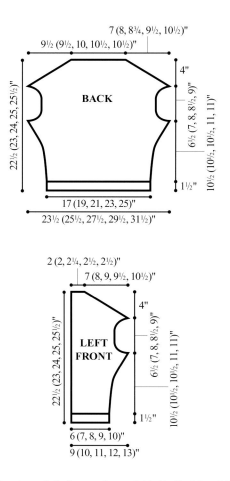

evenly along left front edge—269 (273, 285, 297, 301) sts. Work in seed st for 4½"/11.5cm. Bind off loosely in pat.

Armhole bands

With RS facing and circular needle, pick up and k 79 (85, 97, 103, 109) sts evenly around each armhole edge.

Work in seed st for 1"/2.5cm. Bind off in pat. Sew side and armhole band seams.

Tie

Cast on 18 sts.

Work in k1, p1 rib, slipping first st of every row, until tie measures approx 45 (49, 53, 57, 61)"/114 (124.5, 134.5, 144.5, 155)cm.

Bind off in rib. ■

Cowl Top and Wristers

For a disarmingly charming combo, slip on Annabelle Speer's sleeveless top—knit entirely in simple double-stranded stockinette—with a pair of above-the-elbow wristers. Coordinated ribbing on the gloves and separate cowl puts both these pieces on a parallel track.

SIZES
Top sized for Small, Medium, Large, 1X, 2X and shown in size Small. Wristers in one size.

KNITTED MEASUREMENTS
Top
Bust 34 (38, 42, 46, 50)"/86.5 (96.5, 106.5, 117, 127)cm
Length 23 (23, 23½, 24, 24)"/58.5 (58.5, 60, 61, 61)cm
Cowl
Lower edge circumference 24"/61cm
Length 12½"/31.5cm
Wristers
Circumference (unstretched) 6"/15cm
Length 18½"/47cm

MATERIALS
• 8 (9, 10, 12, 13) 3½oz/100g hanks (each approx 140yd/128m) of HiKoo/Skacel Collection *Simpliworsted* (wool/acrylic/nylon) in #031 real green

• 2 hanks in #029 royal

• One pair size 11 (8 mm) needles OR SIZE TO OBTAIN GAUGE

• One each sizes 11 and 13 (8 and 9mm) circular needles, each 20"/50cm long

STOCKINETTE

23

3¾ (4, 4½, 5, 5)"

6 (6½, 7, 7, 7)"

2"

1½"

FRONT & BACK

21 (21, 21½, 22, 22)"

14"

7½ (7½, 8, 8½, 8½)"

17 (19, 21, 23, 25)"

15 (17, 19, 21, 23)"

• One set (4) size 6 (4mm) double-pointed needles (dpns) OR SIZE TO OBTAIN GAUGE

• Stitch marker and stitch holder

GAUGES

Top

11½ sts and 16 rows = 4"/10cm over St st using size 11 (8mm) needles and 2 strands of yarn held tog.

Cowl

14 sts and 16 rnds = 4"/10cm over rib pat using smaller circular needle.

Wristers

24 sts and 25 rows = 4"/10cm over rib pat using size 6 (4mm) needles.

TAKE TIME TO CHECK GAUGES.

K1, P2 RIB

(multiple of 3 sts)

Rnd 1 (RS) *K1, p2; rep from *.

Rep rnd 1 for k1, p2 rib.

NOTE

Top and cowl are worked with 2 strands of yarn held tog throughout.

BACK

With straight needles and 2 strands of yarn held tog, cast on 49 (55, 60, 66, 72) sts. Work in St st (k on RS, p on WS) until piece measures 4½"/11.5cm from beg, end with a WS row.

Side shaping

Dec row (RS) K2, k2tog, k to last 4 sts, ssk, k2. Rep dec row every 6th row twice more—43 (49, 54, 60, 66) sts. Work even until piece measures 10"/25.5cm from beg, end with a WS row.

Inc row (RS) K2, M1, k to last 2 sts, M1, k2. Rep inc row every 6th row twice more—49 (55, 60, 66, 72) sts. Work even until piece measures 14"/35.5cm from beg, end with a WS row.

Armhole shaping

Dec row (RS) Sl 1, k1, k2tog, k to last 4 sts, ssk, k2.

Next row (WS) Sl 1, p to end.

Rep last 2 rows 4 (5, 6, 8, 11) times more—39 (43, 46, 48, 48) sts. Work even, cont to sl first st of each row, until armhole measures 7½ (7½, 8, 8½, 8½)"/19 (19, 20.5, 21.5, 21.5)cm, end with a WS row.

Shoulder shaping

Bind off 4 (4, 4, 5, 5) sts at beg of next 4 (6, 4, 4, 4) rows, then 3 (0, 5, 4, 4) sts at beg of next 2 rows. Bind off rem 17 (19, 20, 20, 20) sts for back neck.

FRONT

Work as for back until armhole measures 7 (7, 7½, 8, 8)"/18 (18, 19, 20.5, 20.5)cm, end with a WS row.

Neck shaping

Next row (RS) K14 (15, 16, 17, 17), join another 2 strands of yarn and bind off center 11 (13, 14, 14, 14) sts, k to end. Working both sides at once, work next row even.

Dec row (RS) With first ball of yarn, knit to last 4 sts, ssk, k2; with 2nd ball of yarn, k2, k2tog, k to end. Rep dec row every other row twice more, AT SAME TIME, when armhole measures same as back, shape shoulders as for back.

FINISHING

Block pieces lightly to measurements. Sew shoulder and side seams.

COWL

With smaller circular needle and 2 strands of yarn held tog, cast on 84 sts. Join, taking care not to twist sts, and place marker (pm) for beg of rnd. Work in rib pat as foll:

Rnd 1 *K1, p2; rep from * around.

Rep rnd 1 until piece measures 6"/15cm from beg. Change to larger circular needle and cont in pat as established until piece measures 13"/33cm from beg. Bind off loosely in rib.

WRISTERS

Cast on 36 sts, and divide evenly on dpns. Join, being careful not to twist sts, and place marker (pm) for beg of rnd. Work in k1, p2 rib until piece measures 16"/40.5cm from beg.

Next rnd Work first 6 sts in pat as established, slip these sts to holder for thumb, cont in pat to end of rnd—30 sts.

Next rnd Cast on 6 sts, work to end of rnd—36 sts. Cont in pat until piece measures 18½"/47cm from beg. Bind off in rib.

Thumb

Return 6 thumb sts to dpn, pick up and k 6 sts along cast-on edge of thumb opening—12 sts. Divide sts on dpns and work in pat until thumb measures 1"/2.5cm. Bind off in rib. ◾

Boatneck Sweater

Shiri Mor's rolled-edge pullover gives plenty of breathing space with wide sleeves, an exaggerated boatneck, and raglan shaping.

SIZES

Sized for X-Small, Small, Medium, Large, X-Large, XX-Large and shown in size X-Small.

KNITTED MEASUREMENTS

Bust 33 (37, 41, 45, 49, 53)"/84 (94, 104, 114, 124.5, 134.5)cm

Length 23 (23½, 23½, 25, 25½, 25½)"/58.5 (59.5, 59.5, 63.5, 65, 65)cm

Upper arm 13½ (14½, 15½, 16, 17½, 18½)"/34.5 (37, 39.5, 40.5, 44.5, 47)cm

MATERIALS

• 5 (6, 7, 7, 8, 9) 3½oz/100g skeins (each approx 207yd/189m) of Lion Brand Yarn Company *Cotton-Ease* (cotton/acrylic) in #122 taupe ④

• One pair size 7 (4.5mm) needles OR SIZE TO OBTAIN GAUGE

GAUGE

16 sts and 24 rows = 4"/10cm over St st using size 7 (4.5mm) needles.

TAKE TIME TO CHECK GAUGE.

BACK

Cast on 66 (74, 82, 90, 98, 106) sts. Work in St st for 13½ (13½, 13½, 14½, 14½, 14½)"/34.5 (34.5, 34.5, 37, 37, 37)cm, end with a RS row.

Armhole shaping

Bind off 4 (4, 4, 5, 5, 5) sts at beg of next 2 rows.

Row 1 and all WS rows Purl.

Row 2 K2, p1, k to last 3 sts, p1, k2.

Row 4 (dec) K2, p1, k1, ssk, k to last 6 sts, k2tog, k1, p1, k2. Working in pat as established, rep dec row every 8th row 5 (0, 0, 0, 0, 0) times, every 6th row 0 (3, 0, 0, 0, 0) times, every 4th row 0 (6, 10, 9, 7, 3) times, every other row 0 (0, 2, 6, 11, 19) times—46 (46, 48, 48, 50, 50) sts. Work 10 rows in St st, bind off.

FRONT

Work as for back.

Sleeves

Cast on 42 (42, 46, 46, 48, 48) sts. Work in St st for 3"/7.5cm, ending with a WS row.

Next (inc) row (RS) K1, M1, k to last st, M1, k1. Rep inc row every 4th row 0 (0, 0, 0, 0, 4) times, every 6th row 0 (1, 0, 3, 9, 8) times, every 8th row 0 (6, 7, 5, 1, 0) times, every 10th row 5 (0, 0, 0, 0, 0) times—54 (58, 62, 64, 70, 74) sts. Work even until piece measures 14 (14, 14½, 14½, 15, 15)"/35.5 (35.5, 37, 37, 38, 38)cm from beg.

Shape sleeve cap

Bind off 4 (4, 5, 5, 5) sts at beg of next 2 rows.

Row 1 and all WS rows Purl.

Row 2 K2, p1, k to last 3 sts, p1, k2.

Row 4 (dec) K2, p1, k1, ssk, k to last 6 sts, k2tog, k1, p1, k2. Working in pat as established, rep dec row every 4th row 5 (4, 2, 6, 4, 2) times, every other row 11 (14, 18, 12, 17, 21) times—12 (12, 12, 16, 16, 16) sts.

Work 10 rows in St st, bind off.

FINISHING

Sew raglan sleeve caps to raglan armholes. Sew side and sleeve seams. ∎

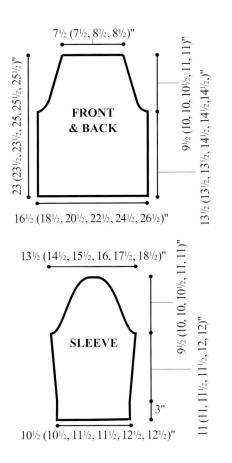

Ruffled Cardi

Tiered stripes of ruffled ribbon yarn anchor Fayla Reiss's reverse-stockinette cardi. Hemmed front bands and a collar that's been picked up, knit and sewn double polish the look.

SIZES

Sized for Small, Medium, Large, 1X, 2X, 3X and shown in size Small.

KNITTED MEASUREMENTS

Bust (closed) 37 (39, 42, 46, 50, 54)"/94 (99, 106.5, 116.5, 127, 137)cm

Length (including bottom ruffle) 22½ (23, 23½, 24, 24½, 25)"/57 (58.5, 59.5, 61, 62, 63.5)cm

Upper arm 12 (13, 14, 15, 16, 17)"/30.5 (33, 35.5, 38, 40.5, 43)cm

MATERIALS

• 4 (5, 5, 6, 7, 7) .88oz/25g balls (each approx 230yd/210m) of Trendsetter Yarns *Kid Seta* (mohair/silk) in #1027 (3)

• 1 (2, 2, 2, 2, 2) 3½oz/100g hanks (each approx 65yd/60m) of Trendsetter Yarns *Cha Cha* (wool/acrylic/nylon) in #433 dark denim (CC)

• One pair size 8 (5mm) needles OR SIZE TO OBTAIN GAUGE

GAUGE

16 sts and 22 rows = 4"/10cm over reverse St st using size 8 (5mm) needles.
TAKE TIME TO CHECK GAUGE.

NOTE

CC is a knitting ribbon. To prepare CC to be worked, open up hank and place on a flat surface or yarn swift. Wind CC around the yarn label, taking care not to fold or twist the ribbon.

RUFFLE PATTERN

Place CC at your left and so horizontal threads that run along one edge of ribbon are at top.

Row 1 (WS) Knit number of sts indicated for piece being made. **To beg ruffle, fold ribbon over toward you so first 2 horizontal threads match up with next 2 horizontal threads. Insert RH needle into next st on LH needle and through first pair of horizontal threads. With MC, knit MC and CC tog. Insert RH needle into next st on LH needle and through next pair of horizontal threads and knit them tog. *Insert RH needle into next st on LH needle and through next horizontal thread and knit them tog; rep from * to number of sts indicated for piece being made. To end ruffle, count 5 horizontal threads from last st worked. Cut through center of ribbon between 5th and 6th horizontal threads. Fold ribbon over toward you so last 2 horizontal threads match up with 2 preceeding horizontal threads. Cont to knit MC and CC tog over next 3 sts.** Knit rem number of sts indicated for piece being made.

Note Use this same technique, for beginning and ending CC, if you need to start a new ball of CC within a row.

Rows 2 and 4 (RS) Purl.

Rows 3 and 5 Knit.

Row 6 Purl.

Rep rows 1–6 for ruffle pat.

BACK

With MC, loosely cast on 72 (76, 82, 90, 98, 106) sts. Purl next row.

Ruffles

Row 1 (WS) K1, rep from ** to ** of ruffle pat to last 4 sts, end k1.

Work to row 6, then rep rows 1–6 five times more, then row 1 once—7 rows of ruffles made. Cont in reverse St st until piece measures 14"/35.5cm from cast-on edge, end with a WS row.

Armhole shaping

Bind off 6 (6, 6, 7, 8, 9) sts at beg of next 2 rows. Dec 1 st each side on next row, then every other row 4 (4, 5, 6, 7, 8) times more—50 (54, 58, 62, 66, 70) sts. Work even until armhole measures 6½ (7, 7½, 8, 8½, 9)"/16.5 (17.5, 19, 20.5, 21.5, 23)cm, end with a WS row.

Neck shaping

Next row (RS) P17 (19, 20, 22, 23, 25), join a 2nd ball of MC and bind off center 16 (16, 18, 18, 20, 20) sts, p to end.

Working both sides at once, dec 1 st from each neck edge on next row, then every row once more. Work even on 15 (17, 18, 20, 21, 23) sts each side until armhole measures 7½ (8, 8½, 9, 9½, 10)"/19 (20.5, 21.5, 23, 24, 25.5)cm, end with a WS row. Bind off each side for shoulders.

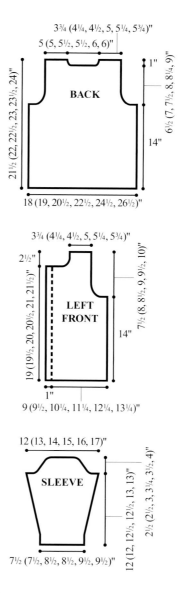

LEFT FRONT

With MC, loosely cast on 40 (42, 45, 49, 53, 57) sts. Purl next row.

Ruffles

Row 1 (WS) K4, rep from ** to ** of ruffle pat to last 4 sts, end k1. Work to row 6, then rep rows 1–6 five times more, then row 1 once—7 rows of ruffles made. Cont in reverse St st until piece measures same length as back to underarm, end with a WS row.

Armhole shaping

Bind off 6 (6, 6, 7, 8, 9) sts at beg of next row. Work next row even.

Dec 1 st from armhole edge on next row, then every other row 4 (4, 5, 6, 7, 8) times more—29 (31, 33, 35, 37, 39) sts. Work even until armhole measures 5 (5½, 6, 6½, 7, 7½)"/12.5 (14, 15, 16.5, 17.5, 19)cm, end with a RS row.

Neck shaping

Next row (WS) Bind off first 11 (11, 12, 12, 13, 13) sts, k to end. Dec 1 st from neck edge on next row, then every other row twice more. Work even on 15 (17, 18, 20, 21, 23) sts until piece measures same length as back to shoulder, end with a WS row. Bind off.

RIGHT FRONT

With MC, loosely cast on 40 (42, 45, 49, 53, 57) sts. Purl next row.

Ruffles

Row 1 (WS) K1, rep from ** to ** of ruffle pat to last 7 sts, end k4. Work to row 6, then rep rows 1-6 five times more, then row 1 once—7 rows of ruffles made.

Cont to work as for left front, reversing all shaping.

SLEEVES

With MC, loosely cast on 30 (30, 34, 34, 38, 38) sts.

Ruffles

Row 1 (WS) K1, rep from ** to ** of ruffle pat to last 4 sts, end k1. Work to row 6, then work row 1

once more—2 rows of ruffles made. Cont in reverse St st and inc 1 st each side on next row, then every 4th row 0 (3, 3, 9, 9, 14) times more, every 6th row 5 (7, 7, 3, 3, 0) times, then every 8th row 3 (0, 0, 0, 0, 0) times—48 (52, 56, 60, 64, 68) sts. Work even until piece measures 12 (12, 12½, 12½, 13, 13)"/30.5 (30.5, 31.5, 31.5, 33, 33)cm from cast-on edge, end with a WS row.

Cap shaping

Bind off 6 (6, 6, 7, 8, 9) sts at beg of next 2 rows. Dec 1 st each side on next row, then every other row 4 (4, 5, 6, 7, 8) times more. Bind off 3 sts at beg of next 4 rows.

Bind off rem 14 (18, 20, 20, 20, 20) sts.

FINISHING

Lightly block pieces to measurements. Sew shoulder seams.

Collar

With RS facing and MC, beg after bound-off sts of right neck, pick up and k 15 sts evenly spaced along right neck edge, 38 (38, 40, 40, 42, 42) sts along back neck edge, then 15 sts along left neck edge—68 (68, 70, 70, 72, 72) sts. Beg with a k row, cont in reverse St st for 7 (7, 7½, 7½, 8, 8)"/17.5 (17.5, 19, 19, 20.5, 20.5)cm. Bind off loosely. Fold collar in half, RS tog. Sew each side edge closed. Turn collar RS out. Sew bound-off edge of collar to WS of neck edge. Set in sleeves. Sew side and sleeve seams, leaving side edges of ruffles unstitched. Turn each front edge 1"/2.5cm to WS and sew in place. ■

Cowl Neck Pullover

Amy Polcyn's loose-fitting sweater is proof that you can smolder without being revealing, with a sheer gold-flecked body and solid cowl and edges.

SIZES

Sized for Small, Medium, Large, 1X, 2X and shown in size Small.

KNITTED MEASUREMENTS

Bust 36 (40, 44, 48, 52)"/91.5 (101.5, 111.5, 122, 132)cm

Length 22½ (23, 24, 25½, 26)"/57 (58.5, 61, 64.5, 66)cm

Upper arm 14 (15, 16, 17, 18)"/35.5 (38, 40.5, 43, 45.5)cm

MATERIALS

• 3 (4, 4, 5, 5) .88oz/25g balls (each approx 230yd/210m) of Schulana/Skacel Collection *Kid Seta Lux* (kid mohair/silk/lurex) in #205 black (MC) **2**

• 4 (5, 5, 6, 6) .88oz/25g balls (each approx 122yd/112m) of Schulana/Skacel Collection *Angora Fashion* (angora/nylon) in #08 black (CC) **3** *

• One pair size 7 (4.5mm) needles OR SIZE TO OBTAIN GAUGES

• Sizes 7, 8, 9, 10, and 10½ (4.5, 5, 5.5, 6, and 6.5mm) circular needles, each 24"/60cm long

• Stitch marker

GAUGES

20 sts and 24 rows = 4"/10cm over St st using MC and size 7 (4.5mm) needles.

24 sts and 28 rows = 4"/10cm over k1, p1 rib using CC and size 7 (4.5mm) needles (unstretched).

TAKE TIME TO CHECK GAUGES.

K1, P1 RIB

(multiple of 2 sts plus 1)

Row 1 (RS) K1, *p1, k1; rep from * to end.

Row 2 P1, *k1, p1; rep from * to end.

Rep rows 1 and 2 for k1, p1 rib.

BACK

With straight needles and CC, cast on 91 (101, 111, 121, 131) sts. Work in k1, p1 rib for 2 (2, 2, 2½, 2½)"/5 (5, 5, 6.5, 6.5)cm, end with a WS row. Change to MC and St st. Work even until piece measures 14 (14, 14½, 15½, 15½)"/35.5 (35.5, 37, 39.5, 39.5)cm from beg.

Armhole shaping

Bind off 6 (7, 8, 9, 10) sts at beg of next 2 rows. Dec 1 st each side on next row, then every other row 5 (6, 7, 9, 10) times more—67 (73, 79, 83, 89) sts. Work even until armhole measures 6½ (7, 7½, 8, 8½)"/16.5 (17.5, 19, 20.5, 21.5)cm, end with a WS row.

* Yarn used in original pattern is no longer available and is listed on page 190.

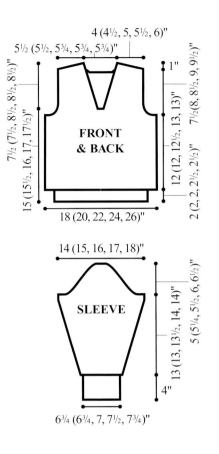

4 (4½, 5, 5½, 6)"

5½ (5½, 5¾, 5¾, 5¾)"

1"

FRONT & BACK

7½ (7½, 8½, 8½, 8½)"

7½ (8, 8½, 9, 9½)"

15 (15½, 16, 17, 17½)"

12 (12, 12½, 13, 13)"

2 (2, 2, 2½, 2½)"

18 (20, 22, 24, 26)"

14 (15, 16, 17, 18)"

SLEEVE

5 (5¼, 5½, 6, 6½)"

13 (13, 13½, 14, 14)"

4"

6¾ (6¾, 7, 7½, 7¾)"

Neck shaping

Next row (RS) Work across first 22 (25, 27, 29, 32) sts, join a 2nd ball of yarn and bind off center 23 (23, 25, 25, 25) sts, work to end. Working both sides at once, work next row even. Dec 1 st from each neck edge on next row, then every other row once more. Work even on 20 (23, 25, 27, 30) sts each side until armhole measures 7½ (8, 8½, 9, 9½)"/19 (20.5, 21.5, 23, 24)cm.

Shoulder shaping

Bind off from each shoulder edge 6 (7, 9, 9, 10) sts once, then 7 (8, 8, 9, 10) sts twice.

FRONT

Work as for back until armhole measures 1 (1½, 1, 1½, 2)"/2.5 (4, 2.5, 4, 5)cm, end with a WS row.

Neck shaping

Next row (RS) Cont armhole shaping, work to center 5 (5, 7, 7, 7) sts, join a 2nd ball of MC and bind off 5 (5, 7, 7, 7) center sts, work to end. Working both sides at once, work next row even. Dec 1 st at each neck edge on next row, then every 4th row 10 times more. When all shaping has been completed, work even on 20 (23, 25, 27, 30) sts each side until piece measures same length as back to shoulder, end with a WS row. Shape shoulders as for back.

SLEEVES

With CC, cast on 41 (41, 43, 45, 47) sts. Work in k1, p1 rib for 4"/10cm, end with a WS row. Change to MC and St st. Inc 1 st each side on next row, then every other row 0 (0, 0, 0, 4) times more, every 4th row 7 (13, 18, 19, 17) times, then every 6th row 7 (3, 0, 0, 0) times—71 (75, 81, 85, 91) sts. Work even until piece measures 17 (17, 17½, 18, 18)"/43 (43, 44.5, 45.5, 45.5)cm from beg, end with a WS row.

Cap shaping

Bind off 6 (7, 8, 9, 10) sts at beg of next 2 rows. Dec 1 st each side on next row, then every other row 5 (6, 7, 8, 9) times more, then every row 14 times. Bind off 2 sts at beg of next 4 rows. Bind off rem 11 (11, 13, 13, 15) sts.

FINISHING

Lightly block pieces to measurements. Sew shoulder seams.

Cowl collar

With RS facing, size 7 (4.5mm) circular needle and CC, beg at right shoulder seam, pick up and k 36 (36, 38, 38, 38) sts evenly spaced along back neck edge to left shoulder seam, 82 (82, 88, 94, 94) sts evenly spaced along front neck edge to right shoulder seam—118 (118, 126, 132, 132) sts. Join and pm for beg of rnd. Work in k1, p1 rib for 3"/7.5cm. Change to size 8 (5mm) circular needle and work in rib for 3"/7.5cm.
Change to size 9 (5.5mm) circular needle and work for 2 (2, 2½, 2½, 2½)"/5 (5, 6.5, 6.5, 6.5)cm.
Change to size 10 (6mm) circular needle and work for 2 (2, 2½, 2½, 2½)"/5 (5, 6.5, 6.5, 6.5)cm.
Change to size 10½ (6.5mm) circular needle and work until collar measures 11 (11, 12, 13, 13)"/28 (28, 30.5, 33, 33)cm from beg. Bind off very loosely in rib. Set in sleeves. Sew side and sleeve seams. ■

Vintage Mohair Sweater

Mohair lends a touch of luxury to this cushy turtleneck. The wide cowl (it's made separately and sewn on), patch pockets, and cuffs bring texture in the form of a twist-stitch garter rib.

SIZES

Sized for X-Small, Small, Medium, Large, X-Large, 2X and shown in size Small.

KNITTED MEASUREMENTS

Bust 32 (36, 40, 44, 48, 52)"/81 (91.5, 101.5, 111.5, 122, 132)cm
Length 22½ (23, 23½, 24, 24½, 25)"/57 (58.5, 59.5, 61, 62, 63.5)cm
Upper arm 14½ (15, 15½, 17, 17½, 18)"/37 (38, 40, 43, 44.5, 45.5)cm

MATERIALS

• 6 (7, 8, 9, 10, 10) 1¾oz/50g balls (each approx 120yd/110m) of Be Sweet *Brushed Mohair* (baby mohair) in burnt red **⑤**

• One pair each sizes 8 and 9 (5 and 5.5mm) needles OR SIZE TO OBTAIN GAUGE

GAUGE

14 sts and 18 rows = 4"/10cm over St st using larger needles.
TAKE TIME TO CHECK GAUGE.

RIB STITCH

(multiple of 4 sts plus 3)
Row 1 (RS) *P1, k1tbl, p1, k1; rep from * to last 3 sts, p1, k1tbl, p1.
Row 2 *K1, p1tbl, k2; rep from * to last 3 sts, k1, p1tbl, k1.
Rep these 2 rows for rib stitch.

BACK

With smaller needles, cast on 56 (63, 70, 77, 84, 91) sts. Work 4 rows in St st. Knit next row on WS for turning ridge. Change to larger needles and work in St st until piece measures 14"/35.5cm from turning ridge, end with a WS row.

Armhole shaping

Bind off 3 (3, 3, 4, 4, 4) sts at beg of next 2 rows. Dec 1 st each side every other row 2 (4, 6, 6, 8, 10) times—46 (49, 52, 57, 60, 63) sts. Work even until armhole measures 7½ (8, 8½, 9, 9½, 10)"/19 (20.5, 21.5, 23, 24, 25.5)cm.

Shoulder shaping

Bind off 4 (4, 5, 6, 6, 7) sts at beg of next 2 rows, then 4 (5, 5, 6, 7, 7) sts at beg of next 2 rows. Bind off rem 30 (31, 32, 33, 34, 35) sts for back neck.

FRONT

Work as given for back until armhole measures 5½ (6, 6½, 7, 7½, 8)"/14 (15, 16.5, 18, 19, 20.5)cm.

Neck shaping

Next row (RS) K14 (15, 16, 18, 19, 20), join a 2nd ball of yarn and bind off center 18 (19, 20, 21, 22, 23) sts, work to end. Working both sides at once with separate balls of yarn, dec 1 st at each neck edge every row 6 times—8 (9, 10, 12, 13, 14) sts. Work even until armhole measures same as back.

Shoulder shaping

Bind off 4 (4, 5, 6, 6, 7) sts from each shoulder edge once, 4 (5, 5, 6, 7, 7) sts once.

SLEEVES

With smaller needles, cast on 35 (35, 35, 39, 39, 39) sts. Work in rib stitch for 4"/10cm, inc 4 sts on the last WS row—39 (39, 39, 43, 43, 43) sts. Change to larger needles. Work in St st for 6 rows.
Inc row (RS) K1, inc 1 st in next st, knit to last 2 sts, inc 1 st in next st, k1. Rep inc row every 8th (8th, 8th, 8th, 6th, 6th) row 5 (6, 7, 7, 8, 9) times more—51 (53, 55, 59, 61, 63) sts. Work even until piece measures 17½ (17½, 18, 18, 18½, 18½)"/44.5 (44.5, 45.5, 45.5, 47, 47)cm from beg.

Cap shaping

Bind off 3 (3, 3, 4, 4, 4) sts at beg of next 2 rows. Dec 1 st each side every other row 7 (8, 9, 10, 11, 12) times, then every row 9 times—13 sts. Bind off rem sts.

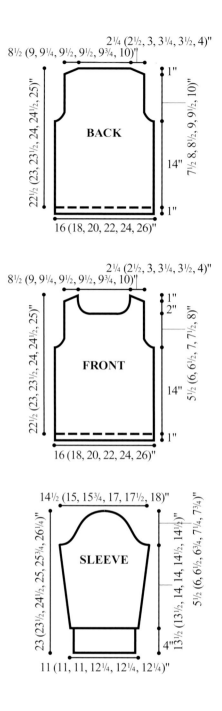

POCKETS (make 2)

With size 9 (5.5mm) needles, cast on 19 sts. Work in rib stitch for 6"/15cm. Bind off in pat.

FINISHING

Sew shoulder seams. Sew side and sleeve seams. Set in sleeves. Turn lower edge of body to WS along turning ridge and sew in place.

Front collar

With larger needles, cast on 71 (71, 75, 75, 79, 79) sts. Work in rib stitch for 8"/20.5cm. Bind off in pat.

Back collar

With larger needles, cast on 55 (59, 59, 63, 63, 63) sts. Work in rib stitch for 8"/20.5cm. Bind off in pat.

Sew collar pieces tog at short edges and sew to neck opening, matching seams to shoulder seams. Fold collar in half to WS and slip st in place. Position and sew pockets using photo as guide. ■

Cropped Tank Top

Scoop-necked and body-skimming with side slits and knit-in finishing details, Jacqueline van Dillen's tank is worked in a knit/purl texture. Extra flair comes from the flamingo colorway.

SIZES

Sized for X-Small, Small, Medium, Large, X-Large and shown in size X-Small.

KNITTED MEASUREMENTS

Bust 31 (33, 35½, 38½, 41)"/78.5 (84, 90, 98, 104)cm
Length 18½ (19, 20, 21, 21½)"/47 (48, 51, 53.5, 54.5)cm

MATERIALS

• 3 (3, 3, 4, 4) 1¾oz/50g hanks (each approx 170yd/160m) of Manos del Uruguay/Fairmount Fibers *Serena* (alpaca/cotton) in #2144 flamingo ②

• One pair size 3 (3.25mm) needles OR SIZE TO OBTAIN GAUGE

• Stitch markers

GAUGES

25 sts and 38 rows = 4"/10cm over chart pat st using size 3 (3.25mm) needles;
25 sts and 36 rows = 4"/10cm over St st using size 3 (3.25mm) needles.
TAKE TIME TO CHECK GAUGES.

BACK

Cast on 96 (104, 112, 120, 128) sts. K 8 rows.

Beg chart

Row 1 (RS) K5, work 8-st rep of chart 10 (11, 12, 13, 14) times, work the last 6 sts of chart, k5.
Cont to foll chart in this way with k5 at beg and end of every row (for garter st-trimmed side slit each side) through row 18 of chart.
Next row K1, work row 1 of chart, working 8-st rep 11 (12, 13, 14, 15) times, work the last 6 sts, k1.
Cont to work chart in this manner until rows 1–36 of chart have been completed twice. Change to St st (k on RS, p on WS) on all sts until piece measures 12 (12, 12½, 13, 13)"/30.5 (30.5, 31.5, 33, 33)cm from beg.

Beg armhole detail

Note The armhole is trimmed with garter sts for a self-finishing effect.
Row 1 and all RS rows Knit.
Row 2 (WS) K6 (6, 7, 8, 8), p to the last 6 (6, 7, 8, 8) sts, k to end.
Row 4 K7 (7, 8, 9, 9), p to the last 7 (7, 8, 9, 9) sts, k to end.
Row 6 K8 (8, 9, 10, 10), p to the last 8 (8, 9, 10, 10) sts, k to end.
Row 8 K9 (9, 10, 11, 11), p to the last 9 (9, 10, 11, 11) sts, k to end.

Armhole shaping

Row 1 (RS) Bind off 4 (4, 5, 6, 6) sts, k to end.

Row 2 (WS) Bind off 4 (4, 5, 6, 6) sts, k5, p to last 6 sts, k6.

Note The decreasing on the foll rows preserves a k6 trim at beg and end of row.

Dec row 3 (RS) Bind off 1 st, k to end.

Dec row 4 (WS) Bind off 1 st, k5, p to last 6 sts, k6. Rep [dec rows 3 and 4] 10 (11, 11, 11, 12) times more—66 (72, 78, 84, 90) sts.

Work even (with k6 trim at beg and end of rows) until armhole measures 4½ (5, 5½, 6, 6½)"/11.5 (12.5, 14, 15, 16.5)cm, end with a RS row.

Beg neckline detail

Row 1 (WS) K6, p15, k24 (30, 36, 42, 48), p15, k6.

Row 2 and all RS rows Knit.

Row 3 (WS) K6, p12, k30 (36, 42, 48, 54), p12, k6.

Row 5 (WS) K6, p to 2 sts before center garter sts, k these sts, k the center garter sts and 2 more sts, p to the last 6 sts, k6.

Rows 7, 9, and 11 Rep row 5.

Neck shaping

Place markers to mark the center 24 (28, 32, 38, 42) sts on the last WS row.

Next row (RS) Work to the marked sts, join a 2nd ball of yarn and bind off center 24 (28, 33, 38, 42) sts, k to end. Cont to work each side separately AND work the neck detail by working 2 more sts each side of neck in garter st until all sts are worked in garter st, AT SAME TIME, bind off 2 sts from each neck edge 4 times, then 1 (2, 3, 3, 4) sts once. Bind off rem 12 sts each side.

FRONT

Work as for back, including the armhole detail and shaping, until armhole measures 1 (1½, 2, 2½, 3)"/2.5 (4, 5, 6.5, 7.5)cm.

Place markers to mark the center 24 (28, 32, 38, 42) sts on the last WS row.

Beg neckline detail

Next row (RS) Bind off 1 st, knit to end.

Next row (WS) Bind off 1 st, k5, purl to the center marked sts, k these sts, p to last 6 sts k6. Cont to work armhole shaping as established, AT SAME TIME, work 1 more st in garter st for the neck detail on each side of the center sts on the next 3 WS rows.

Next row (RS) Bind off 1 st, k to the center 24 (28, 32, 38, 42) sts, join a 2nd ball of yarn and bind off these sts, k to end.

Next row (WS) K6, purl to the last 6 sts on first side, k6; on 2nd side, bind off 1 st, k5, purl to the last 6 sts, k6.

Next row (RS) Bind off 1 st, k to the end of the first side, on 2nd side, bind off 1 st, k to end. Cont to work the neck shaping and the established armhole shaping in this way until there are 12 sts each side in garter st. Work even until armhole measures 6½ (7, 7½, 8, 8½)"/16.5 (18, 19, 20.5, 21.5)cm measured from the first armhole bind-off. Bind off shoulder sts each side.

FINISHING

Block pieces to measurements. Sew shoulder seams. Beg above garter st trim, sew side seams. ■

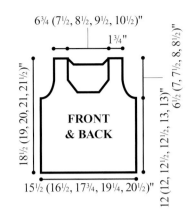

6¾ (7½, 8½, 9½, 10½)"

1¾"

18½ (19, 20, 21, 21½)"

FRONT & BACK

6½ (7, 7½, 8, 8½)"

12 (12, 12½, 12½, 13, 13)"

15½ (16½, 17¾, 19¼, 20½)"

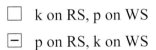

8-st rep

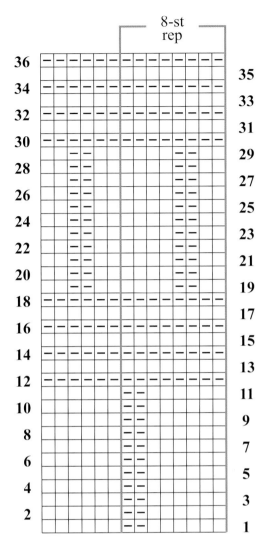

36 34 32 30 28 26 24 22 20 18 16 14 12 10 8 6 4 2

35 33 31 29 27 25 23 21 19 17 15 13 11 9 7 5 3 1

Stitch Key

☐ k on RS, p on WS

⊟ p on RS, k on WS

Pleated Top

Coralie Meslin's swingy top with ruffled cap sleeves and a pleated scoopneck prettily embellished with Crystallized Swarovski Elements was made for a night on the town.

SIZES

Sized for X-Small, Small, Medium, Large, X-Large and shown in size Small.

KNITTED MEASUREMENTS

Bust 33½ (35½, 38½, 41½, 44½)"/85 (90, 97.5, 105.5, 113)cm

Length 22 (22½, 23½, 24½, 25)"/56 (57, 59.5, 62, 63.5)cm

Upper arm 11½ (12½, 13½, 14½, 15½)"/29 (31.5, 34, 37, 39.5)cm

MATERIALS

• 4 (4, 5, 5, 6) .88oz/25g balls (each approx 232yd/212m) of Trendsetter Yarns *Kid Seta* (super kid mohair/silk) in #1015 silver 🔲②

• One pair size 3 (3.25mm) needles OR SIZE TO OBTAIN GAUGE

• Three size 3 (3.25mm) double-pointed needles (dpns) for pleats

• CRYSTALLIZED™ Swarovski Elements

• 1 Large Aquiline Bead (top hole), 28mm size

• 2 Aquiline Beads (top hole), 18mm size

• 4 Pyramids Keystone Beads (two holes), 17x9mm size, style 5181

• 50 (52, 55, 58, 60) Small Pyramids Keystone Beads (two holes), 13x7mm size, style 5181, in #001 GSHA goldenshadow

GAUGE

25 sts and 34 rows = 4"/10cm over St st using size 3 (3.25mm) needles.
TAKE TIME TO CHECK GAUGE.

STITCH GLOSSARY

12-st LP (12-st left pleat) Sl next 4 sts to dpn #1, sl next 4 sts to dpn #2, sl next 4 sts to dpn #3. Hold dpn #1 in front so RS is facing, bring dpn #2 to back so WS is tog with WS of dpn #1. Bring dpn #3 to back so RS is tog with RS of dpn #2. [K 1 st from each dpn tog] 4 times—8 sts dec.

12-st RP (12-st right pleat) Sl next 4 sts to dpn #1, sl next 4 sts to dpn #2, sl next 4 sts to dpn #3. Hold dpn #1 in so RS is facing, bring dpn #2 to front so RS is tog with RS of dpn #1. Bring dpn #3 to front so WS is tog with WS of dpn #2. [K 1 st from each dpn tog] 4 times—8 sts dec.

6-st LP (6-st left pleat) Sl next 2 sts to dpn #1, sl next 2 sts to dpn #2, sl next 2 sts to dpn #3. Hold dpn #1 in front so RS is facing, bring dpn #2 to back so WS is tog with WS of dpn #1. Bring dpn #3 to back so RS is tog with RS of dpn #2. [K 1 st from each dpn tog] twice—4 sts dec.

6-st RP (6-st right pleat) Sl next 2 sts to dpn #1, sl next 2 sts to dpn #2, sl next 2 sts to dpn #3. Hold dpn #1 in so RS is facing, bring dpn #2 to front so RS is tog with RS of dpn #1. Bring dpn #3 to front so WS is tog with WS of dpn #2. [K 1 st from each dpn tog] twice—4 sts dec.

BACK

Cast on 101 (107, 117, 125, 135) sts. Work in garter st for 6 rows. Cont in St st, work even for 10 rows.

Side shaping

Next (dec) row (RS) K2, SKP, k across to last 4 sts, k2tog, k2. Rep dec row every 16th row twice more. Work even on 95 (101, 111, 119, 129) sts until piece measures 8"/20.5cm from beg.
Next (inc) row (RS) K2, M1, k across to last 2 sts, M1, k2. Rep inc row every 16th row twice more. Work even on 101 (107, 117, 125, 135) sts until piece measures 14 (14, 14½, 15, 15)"/35.5 (35.5, 37, 38, 38)cm from beg, end with a WS row.

Armhole shaping

Bind off 3 (3, 4, 5, 6) sts at beg of next 2 rows.
Dec row 1 (RS) K2, SSK, k across to last 4 sts, k2tog, k2.
Dec row 2 (WS) P2, p2tog, p across to last 4 sts, p2tog tbl, p2. Rep last 2 rows twice more, then rep dec row every other row 3 (4, 5, 5, 6) times. Work even on 77 (81, 87, 93, 99) sts until armhole measures 7¼ (7¾, 8¼, 8¾, 9¼)"/18.5 (19.5, 21, 22, 23.5)cm, end with a WS row.

Shoulder and neck shaping

Bind off 7 (8, 8, 9, 10) sts at beg of next 4 rows, then 7 (7, 9, 9, 10) sts at beg of next 2 rows. AT

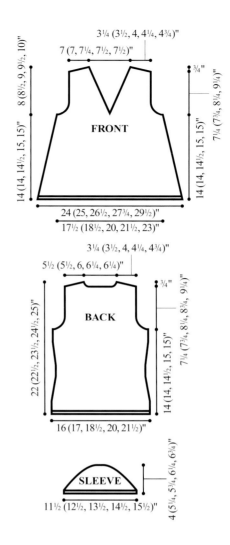

THE SAME TIME, bind off center 27 (27, 29, 31, 31) sts, then, working both sides at once, dec 1 st from each neck edge every row 4 times.

FRONT

Cast on 150 (156, 166, 174, 184) sts. Work in garter st for 6 rows. Cont in St st, work even until piece measures same length as back to underarms.

Armhole and neck shaping

Next row (RS) Bind off 3 (3, 4, 5, 6) sts, k until there are 60 (63, 67, 70, 74) sts on RH needle, 12-st LP, 12-st RP, k to end.

Next row Bind off 3 (3, 4, 5, 6) sts, p to end—128 (134, 142, 148, 156) sts.

Dec row 1 (RS) K2, ssk, k46 (49, 53, 56, 60), 12-st LP, k2tog; join a 2nd ball of yarn, ssk, 12-st RP, k to last 4 sts, k2tog, k2—54 (57, 61, 64, 68) sts each side.

Dec row 2 With first ball of yarn, p2, p2tog, p to end; with 2nd ball of yarn, p to last 4 sts, p2tog tbl, p2.

Dec row 3 (RS) With first ball of yarn, k2, ssk, k to last 8 sts, 6-st LP, k2tog; with 2nd ball of yarn, ssk, 6-st RP, k to last 4 sts, k2tog, k2.

Dec row 4 Rep dec row 2.

Dec row 5 (RS) With first ball of yarn, k2, ssk, k to last 2 sts, k2tog; with 2nd ball of yarn, ssk, k to last 4 sts, k2tog, k2.

Dec row 6 Rep dec row 2. Working same as back, cont to dec 1 st from each armhole edge on next row, then every other row 2 (3, 4, 4, 5) times more. AT THE SAME TIME, dec 1 st from each neck edge on next row, then every other row 10 (8, 8, 8, 6) times more, then every 4th row 8 (10, 11, 12, 14) times. When all shaping has been completed, work even on 21 (23, 25, 27, 30) sts each side until piece measures same length as back to shoulder. Shape shoulders same as back.

SLEEVES

Cast on 72 (78, 84, 90, 96) sts. Work in garter st for 6 rows. Cont in St st as foll:

Cap shaping

Next (dec) row (RS) K2, ssk, k across to last 4 sts, k2tog, k2. Rep dec row every other row 11 (12, 13, 14, 15) times more. Work even on 48 (52, 56, 60, 64) sts until piece measures 4½ (5, 5½, 6, 6½)"/11.5 (12.5, 14, 15, 16.5)cm from beg.

Next (dec) row (RS) *K2tog; rep from * to end—24 (26, 28, 30, 32) sts.

Next (dec) row *P2tog; rep from * to end. Bind off rem 12 (13, 14, 15, 16) sts.

FINISHING

Lightly block pieces to measurements. Sew shoulder seams.

Place markers 6¼ (6¾, 7¼, 7¾, 8¼)"/16 (17, 18.5, 19.5, 21)cm down from shoulders on front and back. Set sleeves into armholes between markers. Sew side seams.

Bead embellishment

Sew large aquiline bead to center front neck, so top of bead is approx ⅛"/.3cm from neck edge. Spacing beads approx ¼"/.5cm apart and ⅛"/.3cm from edge throughout, sew a smaller aquiline bead to each side of large bead. On each side of center group of beads, sew two larger pyramids. Sew smaller keystone beads around rem neck edge. ■

Gathered Cardi

Down to earth yet flirtatious, Cathy Carron's flyaway cardigan is marked by its gathered bodice, seed-stitch collar and borders, and short, full-fashioned raglan sleeves.

SIZES

Sized for X-Small, Small, Medium, Large and shown in size X-Small.

KNITTED MEASUREMENTS

Bust (closed) 32 (35, 38, 41)"/81 (89, 96.5, 104)cm
Length 19¾ (21½, 22½, 23¾)"/50 (54.5, 57, 60.5)cm
Upper arm 12½ (13, 14, 15)"/31.5 (33, 35.5, 38)cm

MATERIALS

• 8 (9, 11, 12) 3½oz/100g hanks (each approx 140yd/128m) of Plymouth Yarn Co. *Fantasy Naturale* (mercerized cotton) in #5228 spring green (4)

• Size 8 (5mm) circular needle, 32"/80cm long, OR SIZE TO OBTAIN GAUGE

• One set (5) size 8 (5mm) double-pointed needles (dpns)

• Stitch markers and holders

• One 1⅜"/35mm button

GAUGE

18 sts and 24 rows = 4"/10cm over St st using size 8 (5mm) circular needle.
TAKE TIME TO CHECK GAUGE.

NOTE

Cardigan is made in one piece from the collar down.

STITCH GLOSSARY

L1 (lift 1) Lift and place horizontal strand between last st made and next st onto LH needle, knit the strand to inc 1 st.

SEED STITCH

Row 1 (RS) *K1, p1; rep from * to end.
Row 2 Knit the p sts and purl the k sts. Rep row 2 for seed st.

COLLAR

With circular needle, cast on 72 (76, 84, 88) sts. Do not join. Work back and forth in seed st for 4"/10cm, end with a WS row.

Yoke

Next row (RS) Work in seed st across first 12 sts (left front band), pm, k4 (5, 7, 8) (left front), pm, k8 (left sleeve), pm, k24 (26, 30, 32) (back), pm, k8 (right sleeve), pm, k4 (5, 7, 8) (right front), pm, work in seed st across last 12 sts (right front band).
Next row Work in seed st across first 12 sts, p to last marker, work in seed st across last 12 sts.
Next (inc) row (RS) Work in seed st across first 12 sts, sl marker, *k to 1 st before next marker, L1, k1, sl marker, k1, L1; rep from * 3 times more, end k to

last marker, sl marker, work in seed st across last 12 sts.

Next row Work in seed st across first 12 sts, p to last marker, work in seed st across last 12 sts. Rep last 2 rows 20 (22, 24, 26) times more.

Next (buttonhole) row (RS) Work inc row to last marker, sl marker, work in seed st across next 4 sts, bind off next 4 sts, work in seed st to end. Work next row even as established, casting on 4 sts over bound-off sts. Cont to work inc row and next row twice more—264 (284, 308, 328) sts.

Divide the yoke

Next row (RS) Work in seed st across first 12 sts, sl marker, k28 (31, 35, 38) (left front), drop marker, place next 56 (60, 64, 68) sts on holders (left sleeve), drop marker, k72 (78, 86, 92) (back), drop marker, place next 56 (60, 64, 68) sts on holders (right sleeve), drop marker, k28 (31, 35, 38) (right front), sl marker, work in seed st across last 12 sts—152 (164, 180, 192) sts.

Next row Work in seed st across first 12 sts, p to last marker, work in seed st across last 12 sts.

BODY

Next (inc) row (RS) Work in seed st across first 12 sts, sl marker, *k next st, from WS insert LH needle into back lp of st 2 rows below st just worked and place on LH needle, k this lp to inc 1 st; rep from * to last st marker, sl marker, work in seed st across last 12 sts—280 (304, 336, 360) sts. Keeping 12 sts each front edge in seed st for front bands and rem sts in St st, work even for 8 (9, 9½, 10)"/20.5 (23, 24, 25.5)cm, end with a WS row.

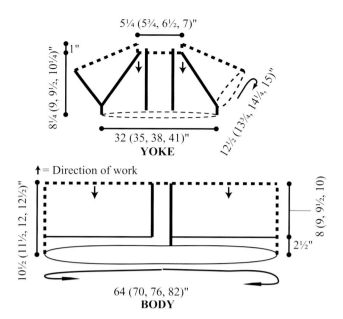

5¼ (5¾, 6½, 7)"

1"

8¼ (9, 9½, 10¼)"

32 (35, 38, 41)"

12½ (13¾, 14¼, 15)"

YOKE

↑ = Direction of work

10½ (11½, 12, 12½)"

8 (9, 9½, 10)

2½"

64 (70, 76, 82)"

BODY

Next row (RS) Work in seed st to end, dropping markers. Cont in seed st for 2½"/6.5cm. Bind off loosely in seed st.

SLEEVES (make two)

With RS facing, dpns and beg at underarm, k56 (60, 64, 68) from left sleeve holders, dividing sts evenly among 4 dpns. Join and pm for beg of rnds.

Next 6 rnds Knit.

Next (dec) rnd K2tog, k to last 2 sts, k2tog.

Rep last 7 rnds once more—52 (56, 60, 64) sts.

Next 3 rnds Knit.

Work the cuff

Next rnd *K1, p1; rep from * around.

Next rnd Knit the p sts and purl the k sts. Rep last rnd for seed st until cuff measures 4"/10cm. Bind off loosely in seed st.

FINISHING

Block piece to measurements. Fold back each cuff 2½"/6.5cm and tack in place at underarm. Sew on button. ∎

Swing Jacket

The outlook is rosy in Vladimir Teriokhin's swingy A-line jacket. Designed to gracefully skim your silhouette, it's knit in reverse stockinette in a pert pink shade.

SIZES

Sized for Small, Medium, Large, X-Large and shown in size Small.

KNITTED MEASUREMENTS

Lower edge (closed) 50 (51½, 54, 58)"/127 (131, 137, 147)cm

Bust (closed) 40 (42, 44½, 48)"/102 (106, 113, 122)cm

Length 25¾ (26½, 26¾, 27¼)"/65.5 (66.5, 68, 69)cm

Upper arm 13½ (14½, 15½, 16½)"/34 (37, 39.5, 42)cm

MATERIALS

• 9 (10, 11, 11) 1¾oz/50g hanks (each approx 131yd/120m) of Rowan/Westminster Fibers *Summer Tweed* (silk/cotton) in #509 sunset ④ *

• One pair each sizes 7 and 8 (4.5 and 5mm) needles OR SIZE TO OBTAIN GAUGE

• Two ⅞"/22mm buttons

GAUGE

18 sts and 22 rows = 4"/10cm over reverse St st using larger needles.
TAKE TIME TO CHECK GAUGE.

BACK

With larger needles, cast on 112 (116, 122, 130) sts. K 8 rows. Then, beg with a purl (RS) row, work in reverse St st, dec 1 st each side every 6th row 11 times—90 (94, 100, 108) sts. Work even until piece measures 14"/35.5cm from beg.

Armhole shaping

Bind off 2 (2, 3, 3) sts at beg of next 2 rows.
Dec row (RS) P1, [p2tog] twice, p to last 5 sts, [p2tog] twice, p1. Rep dec row every 8th row 4 (2, 4, 0) times, every 6th row 2 (5, 3, 9) times—58 (58, 62, 62) sts. Work even until armhole measures 9 (9½, 10, 10½)"/23 (24, 25.5, 26.5)cm.

* Yarn used in original pattern is no longer available and is listed on page 190.

Shoulder shaping

Bind off 6 sts at beg of next 6 (6, 2, 2) rows, 7 sts at beg of next 0 (0, 4, 4) rows. Bind off rem 22 sts for back neck.

LEFT FRONT

With larger needles, cast on 54 (58, 60, 64) sts. K 8 rows. Then, beg with a purl (RS) row, work in reverse St st, dec 1 st at beg of every 6th row 11 times, AT SAME TIME, when piece measures 5½"/14cm from beg, work pocket opening as foll:
Next row (RS) Work 14 sts, bind off 24 sts, work to end. Then, with larger needles, separately cast on 24 sts and work in reverse St st for 9"/23cm (this is the folded-over pocket lining) and leave on hold. Return to main piece on next knit (WS) row, k to the pocket bind-off, knit across the 24 sts on hold, k to end. Cont on all sts as before with dec's as established. After all dec's are completed, there are 43 (47, 49, 53) sts. Work even until piece measures 14"/35.5cm from beg.

Armhole shaping

Note Read before beg to knit.
Next row (RS) Bind off 2 (2, 3, 3) sts, p to end. Work 1 row even.
Dec row (RS) P1, [p2tog] twice, p to end. Rep dec row every 8th row 4 (2, 4, 0) times, every 6th row 2 (5, 3, 9) times, AT SAME TIME, when armhole measures 8½ (9, 9½, 10)"/21.5 (23, 24, 25.5)cm, end with a RS row and work neck shaping as foll:

Neck shaping

Next row (WS) Bind off 5 sts, k to end. Cont to shape neck, binding off 4 sts from each neck edge once, 2 sts twice, AT SAME TIME, when armhole measures 9 (9½, 10, 10½)"/23 (24, 25.5, 26.5)cm, work shoulder shaping as foll:

Shoulder shaping

Bind off 4 sts from armhole edge 2 (4, 3, 3) times, 3 (0, 5, 5) sts 2 (0, 1, 1) times.

RIGHT FRONT

Work as for left front, reversing all shaping and having 24-st pocket placement at 14 sts from side seam.

LEFT SLEEVE

With larger needles, cast on 66 (70, 76, 80) sts. K 8 rows. Beg with a purl (RS) row, work in reverse St st, dec 1 st each side every 10th row 3 times—60 (64, 70, 74) sts. Work even until piece measures 7½"/19cm from beg.

Armhole shaping

Bind off 2 (2, 3, 3) sts at beg of next 2 rows.
Dec row (RS) P1, [p2tog] twice, p to last 5 sts, [p2tog] twice, p1. Rep dec row every 4th row 10 (11, 12, 13) times more—12 sts. Work even on these 12 sts for saddle shoulder until piece fits along front armhole and across top of front shoulder.
***Next row (WS)** Bind off 4 sts, work to end. Work 1 row even. Rep the last 2 rows once more. Bind off rem sts.*

RIGHT SLEEVE

Work as for left sleeve, only reversing shaping at top of cap (between *'s) by beg first bind-off row on RS.

BELT

With smaller needles, cast on 22 sts. Work in k1, p1 rib for 60"/152cm. Bind off in rib.

FINISHING

Block pieces to measurements. Set sleeve into armholes, sewing saddle shoulder extensions across the front and back shoulders. Sew side and sleeve seams. Fold pockets in half and sew the cast-on edge of pocket lining to the 24 sts bound off on the front pocket opening. Seam linings.

Left front band

With larger needles, pick up and k 85 (87, 89, 91) sts evenly along left front edge. Work in garter st for 6 rows. Bind off.

Right front band

Pick up and k sts as for left front band.
Row 1 (WS) K3, (k2tog, yo) for buttonhole, k to end. K 5 rows more. Bind off.

Neckband

With smaller needles, pick up and k 83 sts evenly around neck edge. K 3 rows.
Buttonhole row (RS) K3, (k2tog, yo) for buttonhole, k to end. K 4 rows more. Bind off. Sew on buttons opposite buttonhole. ∎

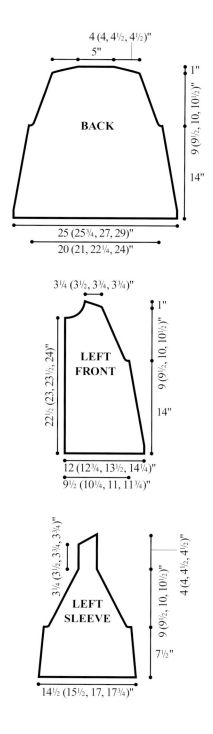

Cardi Vest

From the reverse-stockinette body and exposed seaming to the patch pockets and ribbon yarn, John Brinegar's tailored cardi vest bursts with texture.

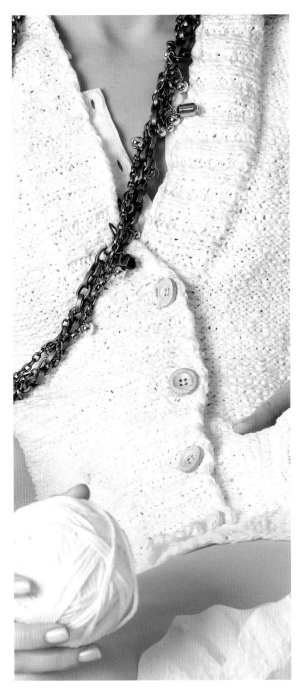

SIZES

Sized for X-Small, Small, Medium, Large, X-Large and shown in size Small.

KNITTED MEASUREMENTS

Bust 32 (36, 41, 44½, 48)"/81 (91.5, 104, 113, 122)cm
Length 26 (27, 28, 28½, 29½)"/66 (68.5, 71, 72.5, 75)cm

MATERIALS

• 8 (9, 9, 10, 11) 1¾oz/50g skeins (each approx 100yd/91m) of Trendsetter *Dolcino* (acrylic/nylon) in #112 stark white ④

• One pair each sizes 10 and 10½ (6 and 6.5mm) needles OR SIZE TO OBTAIN GAUGE

• Size 10 (6mm) circular needle, 32"/80cm long

• Stitch markers and holders

• Scrap yarn and crochet hook

• Five 1"/2.5cm buttons

GAUGE

18 sts and 25 rows = 4"/10cm over St st using larger needles.
TAKE TIME TO CHECK GAUGE.

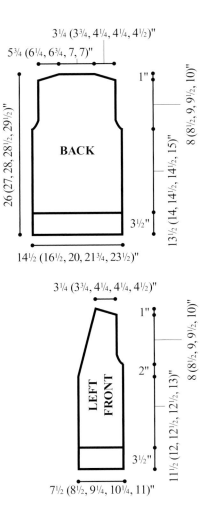

3¼ (3¾, 4¼, 4¼, 4½)"

5¾ (6¼, 6¾, 7, 7)"

1"

BACK

26 (27, 28, 28½, 29½)"

8 (8½, 9, 9½, 10)"

13½ (14, 14½, 14½, 15)"

3½"

14½ (16½, 20, 21¾, 23½)"

3¼ (3¾, 4¼, 4¼, 4½)"

1"

2"

LEFT FRONT

8 (8½, 9, 9½, 10)"

11½ (12, 12½, 12½, 13)"

3½"

7½ (8½, 9¼, 10¼, 11)"

SHORT ROW WRAP & TURN (w&t)

Instructions given for RS row; WS row in parentheses.

1) Wyib (wyif), sl next st purlwise.

2) Move yarn between the needles to the front (back).

3) Sl the same st back to LH needle. Turn work. One st is wrapped.

When working the wrapped st, insert RH needle under the wrap and work it tog with the corresponding st on needle.

BACK

With smaller needles, cast on 66 (74, 90, 98, 106) sts.

Row 1 (RS) K3, *p2, k2; rep from * to last 3 sts, p3.

Row 2 K the knit st and p the purl sts. Work in rib as established for 3½"/9cm, end with a WS row. Change to larger needles.

Row 1 (RS) Sl 1, p to last st, k1.

Row 2 Sl 1, k to end of row. Work even in rev St st, maintaining selvage sts as established, until piece measures 17 (17½, 18, 18, 18½)"/43 (44.5, 45.5, 45.5, 47)cm from beg, end with a WS row. Place markers at each side of last row worked.

Armhole shaping

Row 1 (RS) Sl 1, k2, p2tog, p to last 5 sts, p2tog, k3.

Row 2 Sl 1, p2, k to last 3 sts, p2, k1. Rep last 2 rows 4 (5, 10, 13, 15) times more—56 (62, 68, 70, 74) sts.

Next row (RS) Sl 1, k2, p to last 3 sts, k3.

Next row Sl 1, p2, k to last 3 sts, p2, k1. Work even as established until piece measures 25 (26, 27, 27½, 28½)"/63.5 (66, 68.5, 70, 72.5)cm from beg, end with a WS row.

Shoulder shaping

Short row 1 (RS) Sl 1, k2, purl to last 5 (5, 6, 6, 7) sts, w&t.

Short row 2 (WS) K to last 5 (5, 6, 6, 7) sts, w&t.

Short row 3 P to last 15 (17, 19, 19, 21) sts, w&t.

Short row 4 K to last 15 (17, 19, 19, 21) sts, w&t.

Short row 5 P to last 3 sts, hiding all wraps, k3.

Next row Sl 1, p2, k to last 3 sts, hiding wraps, p2, k1. Bind off in pat.

LEFT FRONT

With smaller needles, cast on 34 (38, 42, 46, 50) sts.

Row 1 (RS) K3, *p2, k2; rep from *, end p3.

Row 2 K the knit sts and p the purl sts. Work in rib pat as established for 3½"/9cm, end with a WS row. Change to larger needles.

Row 1 Sl 1, p to end.

Row 2 Knit. Work even in rev St st, maintaining selvage st, until piece measures 15 (15½, 16, 16, 16½)"/38 (39.5, 40.5, 40.5, 42)cm from beg, end with a WS row.

Neck and armhole shaping

Dec row (RS) P to the last 3 sts, p2tog, p1. Rep dec row every 4th row 11 (12, 2, 2, 1) times more, every 6th row 2 (2, 9, 10, 11) times, AT SAME TIME, when piece is same length as back to armhole, pm and shape armhole at beg of RS rows as for back. After all shaping is complete, cont on rem 15 (17, 19, 19, 21) sts until armhole measures same length as back to shoulder. Shape shoulder at side edge as for back.

RIGHT FRONT

With smaller needles, cast on 34 (38, 42, 46, 50) sts.

Row 1 (RS) P3, *k2, p2; rep from *, end k3.

Row 2 K the knit sts and p the purl sts. Work in rib pat as established for 3½"/9cm, end with a WS row. Change to larger needles.

Complete as for left front, reversing all shaping.

POCKETS (make 2)

With larger needles, cast on 18 sts. Beg with a purl (WS) row, work 24 rows in St st, then 4 rows in rev St st, end with a RS row. Bind off knitwise.

FINISHING

Sew shoulder seams so that seam shows on RS. Sew side seams from lower edge to end of ribbing so that seam shows on WS, then sew to marker at beg of armhole shaping so that seam shows on RS. Sew pockets to fronts, 4½"/11.5cm from lower edge and 2"/5cm in from front edge.

RIBBED BAND

With RS facing and circular needle, pick up and k 108 (111, 116, 119, 123) sts evenly along right center front edge to shoulder, pick up and k 30 (32, 34, 36, 36) sts across back neck, pick up and k 108 (111, 116, 119, 123) sts evenly along left center front edge to lower edge—246 (254, 266, 274, 282) sts.

Next row (WS) P2, *k2, p2; rep from * to end. Cont in k2, p2 rib for 2"/5cm, end with a WS row.

Next (buttonhole) row K2, p2, k2, bind off 2 sts, *rib 10 (10, 10, 12, 12) sts, bind off 2 sts; rep from * 4 times more, rib to end.

Next row Work in rib, casting on 2 sts over bound-off sts. Work 2 more rows in rib. Bind off sts in pat.

Sew buttons to right front opposite buttonholes. ∎

Boatneck Top

Cathy Carron's gathered-bodice tank exudes a come-hither sunniness with its deep ribbed waistband that burgeons into a stockinette yoke and a ribbon tied at its wide split neck.

SIZES

Sized for X-Small, Small, Medium, Large, X-Large, XX-Large and shown in size X-Small.

KNITTED MEASUREMENTS

Bust 33½ (37½, 41½, 45½, 49½, 53½)"/85 (95, 105.5, 115.5, 125.5, 136)cm

Length 18½ (19, 19½, 21, 21½, 22)"/47 (48, 49.5, 53.5, 54.5, 56)cm

MATERIALS

• 4 (5, 5, 6, 7, 8) 1¾oz/50g balls (each approx 103yd/94m) of Classic Elite Yarns *Chesapeake* (organic cotton/merino) in #5950 goldenrod (**4**)*

• One size 7 (4.5mm) circular needle, 24"/60cm long, OR SIZE TO OBTAIN GAUGE

• 2yd/2m ¼"/6.5mm ribbon or cording

• Stitch holders

GAUGE

20 sts and 26 rows = 4"/10cm over St st.
TAKE TIME TO CHECK GAUGE.

BODY

Cast on 120 (140, 160, 180, 200, 220) sts. Place marker and join for knitting in the round. Work in k2, p2 rib for 10 (10, 10, 11, 11, 11)"/25.5 (25.5,

* Yarn used in original pattern is no longer available and is listed on page 190.

LIGHT & EASY

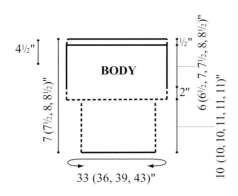

4½"

½"

BODY

2"

7 (7½, 8, 8½)"

6 (6½, 7, 7½, 8, 8½)"

10 (10, 10, 11, 11, 11)"

33 (36, 39, 43)"

25.5, 28, 28, 28)cm, increasing 48 sts evenly around on last row—168 (188, 208, 228, 248, 268) sts. Change to St st and work until piece measures 12 (12, 12, 13, 13, 13)"/30.5 (30.5, 30.5, 33, 33, 33)cm.

Separate for front and back

Next row (RS) K 88 (98, 108, 118, 128, 138) sts for front, place 80 (90, 100, 110, 120, 130) sts for back on holder.

Front

Row 2 (WS) Sl 1, k1, p to last 2 rows, k2.

Row 3 (RS) Sl 1, k to end. Rep rows 2 and 3 until armhole measures 3½ (4, 4½, 5, 5½, 6)"/9 (10, 11.5, 12.5, 14, 15)cm, end with a WS row.

Next row (RS) Sl 1, k1, k42 (47, 52, 57, 62, 67), attach second ball of yarn and knit to end. Working both sides at once and maintaining sl sts at armhole and neck edge, work until armhole measures 6 (6½, 7, 7½, 8, 8½)"/15 (16.5, 18, 19, 20.5, 21.5)cm. Place sts on holder.

Back

Row 2 (WS) Sl 1, k1, p to last 2 rows, k2.

Row 3 (RS) Sl 1, k to end. Rep rows 2 and 3 until armhole measures 6 (6½, 7, 7½, 8, 8½)"/15 (16.5, 18, 19, 20.5, 21.5)cm. Break yarn.

Join front and back

Row 1 With WS facing and beg at left front neck edge, sl 1, k across left front neck, back neck, right front neck.

Row 2 (RS) Sl 1, k1, *yo, k2tog; rep from * to last 2 sts, k2.

Rows 3 and 4 Sl 1, k to end. Bind off knitwise on WS.

FINISHING

Weave ribbon through eyelets and tie at front neck. ◼

Cutout Pullover

The subtle natural variations of the yarn lend depth to Kristin Omdahl's cutout top, worked in the round from the garter-stitch bottom up.

SIZES

Sized for Small, Medium, Large, X-Large and shown in size Medium.

KNITTED MEASUREMENTS

Bust 34 (36, 38, 40)"/86.5 (91.5, 96.5, 101.5)cm
Length 21¾ (22, 22¼, 22¾)"/55 (56, 56.5, 58)cm
Upper arm 13¼ (14, 14½, 15½)"/33.5 (35.5, 37, 39.5)cm

MATERIALS

• 9 (9, 10, 11) 1¾oz/50g balls (each approx 115yd/ 105m) of Be Sweet *Bamboo* (bamboo) in #622 sage ⓛ3

• Size 3 (3.25mm) circular needles, one each 24"/60cm and 16"/40cm long, OR SIZE TO OBTAIN GAUGE

• Stitch markers

GAUGE

24 sts and 32 rows = 4"/10cm over St st using size 3 (3.25mm) needles.
TAKE TIME TO CHECK GAUGE.

BODY

With longer circular needle, cast on 204 (216, 228, 240) sts. Place marker for beg of rnd and join, being careful not to twist sts.
Rnd 1 K102 (108, 114, 120), pm (for side seam), k to end of rnd.

Rnd 2 Purl. Cont in garter st (k 1 rnd, p 1 rnd) as established until piece measures 2"/5cm from beg. Then, work in St st (k every rnd) until piece measures 15"/38cm from beg.

Separate at armhole

Next rnd Bind off 3 sts, k to 3 sts before side seam marker, bind off 3 sts, remove marker, bind off 3 sts, k to last 3 sts, with separate length of yarn, bind off 3 sts. There are 96 (102, 108, 114) sts each for front and for back. Leave the first sts on holder to be worked later for front.

BACK

Work back and forth on 96 (102, 108, 114) sts as foll:
Row 1 (WS) Purl.
Dec row 2 (RS) K1, ssk, k to the last 3 sts, k2tog, k1.
Rep last 2 rows 2 (2, 3, 5) times more—90 (96, 100, 102) sts. Work even in St st (k on RS, p on WS) until armhole measures 6½ (6¼, 6¾, 7¼)"/16 (16.5, 17, 18.5)cm, end with a RS row.
Next row (WS) P21 (24, 26, 27), k 48 center sts (for neck), p21 (24, 26, 27). Cont to work the shoulder sts in St st AND the center 48 sts in garter st (k every row), until armhole measures 6¾ (7, 7¼, 7¾)"/17 (18, 18.5, 19.5)cm.
Last row Work 21 (24, 26, 27) sts, bind off center 48 sts, work rem sts. Leave the shoulder sts on hold for binding off with the front shoulders in the finishing.

FRONT

Work as for back until the armhole shaping is completed—90 (96, 100, 102) sts. Work even for 1 (3, 3, 3) rows more.

Flower cutout

Next row (RS) K42 (45, 47, 48), join a 2nd ball of yarn and bind off center 6 sts, k to end. Working both sides at once with separate balls of yarn, work even until piece measures 3"/7.5cm from the 6-st bind-off.

Next row (RS) K sts of first side, cast on 6 sts, k sts of 2nd side—90 (96, 100, 102) sts. P 1 row on all sts.

Next row (RS) K21 (24, 26, 27), join a 2nd ball of yarn and bind off center 48 sts, k to end. Working both sides at once with separate balls of yarn, work even for 2"/5cm from the 48-st bind-off.

Next row (RS) K the first side, cast on 48 sts, k sts of the 2nd side. P 1 row on all sts.

Next row (RS) K42 (45, 47, 48), *insert RH needle under the 6 cast-on sts from the rows below and pick up a loop to place on LH needle, then k next st on LH needle and pass the picked-up loop over and off the needle; rep from * until all 6 sts are worked, k to end. Work even in St st for 6 rows more.

Next row (WS) P21 (24, 26, 27), k 48 center sts, p21(24, 26, 27). Cont to work the shoulder sts in St st AND the center 48 sts in garter st until armhole measures same as back.

Last row Using the 3-needle bind-off method, join 21 (24, 26, 27) sts of one shoulder with the matching back shoulder, bind off center 48 sts, join the rem shoulder st to the back shoulder.

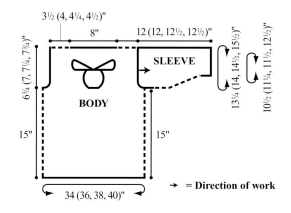

3½ (4, 4¼, 4½)"
8"
12 (12, 12½, 12½)"
6¾ (7, 7¼, 7¾)"
13¼ (14, 14½, 15½)"
10½ (11¼, 11½, 12½)"
SLEEVE
BODY
15"
15"
34 (36, 38, 40)"
➔ = Direction of work

SLEEVES

Note Sleeves are picked up around the armhole edge and worked in rounds to the cuff edge. With shorter circular needle, from the RS and beg at the armhole edge, above the bind-off, pick up and k 40 (42, 44, 47) sts to the shoulder, then 40 (42, 44, 47) sts along the other armhole edge. Do not join; turn work.

Row 1 (WS) Purl to the bound-off st, pick up and purl this st, then pass the last sleeve st over this st and off the needle.

Row 2 Knit and rep row 1.

Rep these 2 rows until all bound-off armhole sts are joined. There are 80 (84, 88, 94) sts. Join to work in the round and pm to mark beg of rnd. Work in rnds of St st for 5"/12.5cm.

Dec rnd K1, k2tog, k to the last 3 sts, ssk, k1. K 3 rnds. Rep the last 4 rnds 7 (7, 8, 8) times more—64 (68, 70, 76) sts. K 12 rnds.

Split the cuff

Next row (RS) Bind off 1 st, k to end. Work in rows of garter st for 1½"/4cm. Bind off. Rep for other sleeve. ■

Drop Stitch Pleated Top

Cathy Carron's airy sleeveless pleated tank is worked circularly in one piece from the hemline to the armholes. The skirt is composed in a drop stitch pattern, and the ribbed bodice sports an eyelet detail in the back.

SIZES

Sized for Small, Medium, Large, X-Large and shown in size Small.

KNITTED MEASUREMENTS

Bust (unstretched) 26¼ (27¾, 29½, 31)"/67 (70.5, 75, 79)cm

Length 22½ (23½, 24¾, 25¾)"/57 (59.5, 63, 65.5)cm

MATERIALS

• 6 (6, 7, 8) 1¾oz/50g balls (each approx 109yd/100m) of Zitron/Skacel Collection *Savanna* (cotton/linen/rayon) in #11 pale rose ③

• Size 6 (4mm) circular needle, 24"/60cm long, OR SIZE TO OBTAIN GAUGES

• One pair size 6 (4mm) needles for 3-needle bind-off

• Two stitch markers, stitch holder

GAUGES

17 sts and 30 rows = 4"/10cm over St st (after dropping every 6th st), using size 6 (4mm) needle.

25 sts and 28 rows = 4"/10cm over k1, p1 rib (unstretched) using size 6 (4mm) needle.

TAKE TIME TO CHECK GAUGES.

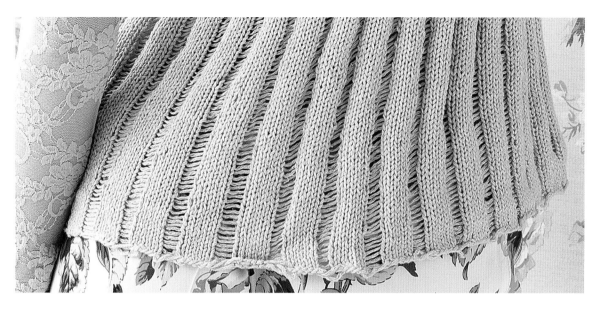

NOTES

1) Tank is worked in the round to underarm, then divided, and front and back are worked separately back and forth in rows.

2) Due to the nature of k1, p1 rib fabric, the finished bust measurement, unstretched, may seem small, but it will stretch to fit when worn.

STITCH GLOSSARY

Visible Inc (VI) Insert LH needle from front to back under the horizontal strand between last st worked and next st on LH needle. K into the front loop for an untwisted (open) inc.

BODY—SKIRT

Cast on 198 (210, 222, 234) sts. Place marker (pm), and join. K every rnd for 8½ (9, 9½, 10)"/21.5 (23, 24, 25.5)cm.

Next rnd *K5, drop next st from LH needle; rep from * around—165 (175, 185, 195) sts. Gently help the dropped sts unravel or "run" down the fabric by stretching or pulling the fabric downward.

Next rnd K2tog, k to end of rnd—164 (174, 184, 194) sts.

Bodice

Work in k1, p1 rib for 7¼"/18.5cm.

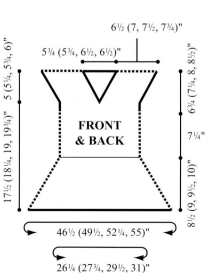

6½ (7, 7½, 7¾)"

5¾ (5¾, 6½, 6½)"

5 (5¼, 5¾, 6)"

6¾ (7¼, 8, 8½)"

17½ (18¼, 19, 19¾)"

FRONT & BACK

7¼"

8½ (9, 9½, 10)"

46½ (49½, 52¼, 55)"

26¼ (27¾, 29½, 31)"

Divide for front and back

Next rnd Work 82 (88, 92, 98) sts (for front), place rem 82 (86, 92, 96) sts on a holder (for back).

FRONT

Work back and forth in rows on front sts for 11 (13, 15, 17) more rows. Armhole measures approx 1¾ (2, 2¼, 2½)"/4.5 (5, 5.5, 6.5)cm.

Divide for neck

Next row (RS) Rib 41 (44, 46, 49) sts, join 2nd ball of yarn, rib to end. Working both sides at same time, work even until armhole measures 6¾ (7¼, 8, 8½)"/17 (18.5, 20.5, 21.5)cm. Place shoulder sts each side on 2 separate holders. Cut yarn.

BACK

With RS facing, rejoin yarn and work in rib pat as established over 82 (86, 92, 96) sts of back until armhole measures same length as front to neck, end with a WS row.

Shape V-inset

Next row (RS) Rib 41 (43, 46, 48) sts, pm, VI, pm, rib to end—83 (87, 93, 97) sts.

***Next row (WS)** Rib to marker, sl m, p1, sl m, rib to end.

Next row (RS) Rib to marker, VI, sl m, k1, sl m, VI, rib to end—85 (89, 95, 99) sts.

Rep from * (working inc sts into rib pat) 16 (17, 18, 19) times more—117 (123, 131, 137) sts. Work 1 WS row. Do not cut yarn. Leave sts on needle. Turn garment inside out. Place front sts onto a straight needle. Holding needles tog, join shoulders, using 3-needle bind-off (and other straight needle), as foll: [k first st from each needle tog] twice, pass first st on RH needle over 2nd st and off needle, *k next 2 sts tog, pass first st over 2nd st; rep from * until all sts of first shoulder have been used. Cont to bind off back neck sts as foll: k1, pass first st over 2nd st, [k2tog, pass first st over 2nd st] 17 (17, 19, 19) times, join 2nd shoulder, using 3-needle bind-off as before.

FINISHING

Block piece. Weave in ends. ■

Waist Tie Tunic

Mod and merry, Jacqueline van Dillen's tunic cape wears its deconstruction well. The exposed center and side seams result when the four stockinette pieces are sewn together.

SIZES

Sized for Small, Medium, Large, 1X, 2X and shown in size Medium.

KNITTED MEASUREMENTS

Bust 38 (40, 43, 47, 50)"/96.5 (101.5, 109, 119, 127)cm

Hip 44 (47, 50, 53, 56)"/111.5 (119, 127, 134, 142)cm

Length 32½ (33, 33½, 34, 34½)"/82.5 (84, 85, 86, 87.5)cm

MATERIALS

• 8 (8, 9, 10, 10) 1¾oz/50g hanks (each approx 110yd/101m) of Classic Elite Yarns *Majestic Tweed* (angora/silk/nylon) in #7258 cherry pie (A) **4** *

• 4 (4, 5, 5, 5) 1¾oz/50g balls (each approx 225yd/206m) of Classic Elite Yarns *Giselle* (wool/mohair/nylon) in #4158 alhambra red (B) **4**

• One pair size 6 (4mm) needles OR SIZE TO OBTAIN GAUGE

• Size 6 (4mm) circular needles, one each 24"/60cm and 16"/40cm long

• Stitch marker

GAUGE

13 sts and 19 rows = 4"/10cm over St st using 1 strand each A and B held tog and size 6 (4mm) needles.

TAKE TIME TO CHECK GAUGE.

NOTES

1) Work with 1 strand each A and B held tog, unless otherwise specified.

2) All seams are put together using mattress st on the WS of the garment for an exposed seam effect on the RS of piece.

3) Garment is made from the top down.

RIGHT BACK

Beg at the neck edge, with 1 strand each A and B held tog and size 6 (4mm) needles, cast on 15 (17, 17, 18, 18) sts.

Row 1 (RS) Knit.

Inc row 2 (WS) P1, pfb, p to end.

Rep last 2 rows 11 (11, 13, 15, 18) times more—27 (29, 31, 34, 37) sts.

**Cont in St st, rep inc row 2 every 10th row 4 times. Work 8 rows even.

Next row (RS) K15 (16, 17, 19, 20), (k2tog, yo) for tie opening, k to end.

Next row (WS) Rep inc row 2. Then cont to rep inc row 2 every 10th row 4 times more—36 (38, 40,

* Yarn used in original pattern is no longer available and is listed on page 190.

43, 46) sts. Work even until piece measures 31 (31½, 32, 32½, 33)"/78.5 (80, 81, 82.5, 84)cm from beg.

Hem
Drop 1 strand of A and cont to work in St st with B only for 8 rows. Bind off.

LEFT BACK
Cast on as for right back.

Row 1 (RS) Knit.

Inc row 2 (WS) P to last 2 sts, pfb, p1.

Rep last 2 rows 11 (11, 13, 15, 18) times more— 27 (29, 31, 34, 37) sts.

**Cont in St st, rep inc row 2 every 10th row 4 times. Work 8 rows even.

Next row (RS) K14 (15, 16, 17, 19), (k2tog, yo) for tie opening, k to end.

Next row (WS) Rep inc row 2. Then cont to rep inc row 2 every 10th row 4 times more—36 (38, 40, 43, 46) sts. Complete as for right back.

LEFT FRONT
Beg at the neck edge with 1 strand A and B held tog, cast on 2 sts.

Row 1 (RS) K1, kfb (for neck inc).

Row 2 (WS) P1, pfb (for armhole inc), p to end.

Row 3 K1, kfb (for neck inc), k to end.

Rep rows 2 and 3 for 3 (5, 5, 6, 6) times more.

Next row (WS) Rep inc row 2.

Next row (RS) Cast on 2 sts, k to end.

Rep last 2 rows 3 times more—23 (27, 27, 29, 29) sts. Then rep armhole inc only every WS row 4 (2, 4, 5, 8) times—27 (29, 31, 34, 37) sts. Then, beg at **, complete as for right back.

RIGHT FRONT

Beg at neck edge with 1 strand A and B held tog, cast on 2 sts.

Row 1 (RS) K1, kfb (for neck inc).

Row 2 (WS) P1, p to last 2 sts, pfb, p1.

Row 3 K to last 2 st, kfb, k1.

Rep rows 2 and 3 for 3 (5, 5, 6, 6) times more.

Next row (WS) Cast on 2 sts, p to last 2 sts, pfb, p1.

Next row (RS) Knit.

Rep last 2 rows 3 times more. Then rep armhole inc only every WS row until there are 27 (29, 31, 34, 37) sts. Then, beg at **, complete as for left back.

FINISHING

Seam the 2 pieces for back at the center, working from the WS so that the seam shows on the RS (see note). Seam the front in same way. Place markers at 13½"/34cm from lower edge and sew one side seam with the same exposed seam method. Leave an opening of 9 (9, 9½, 10, 10)"/23 (23, 24, 25.5, 25.5)cm at the armhole and seam the shoulders in same way.

Armhole trims

With RS facing, 16"/40cm circular needle and 1 strand B, pick up and k 48 (48, 51, 54, 54) sts evenly around armhole opening. Join and k 8 rnds. Bind off.

Tie

With 1 strand A and B held tog, cast on 5 sts. Work in St st for approx 57"/145cm. Bind off.

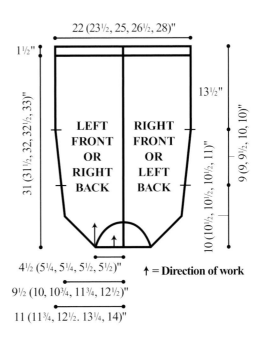

22 (23½, 25, 26½, 28)"

1½"

31 (31½, 32, 32½, 33)"

LEFT FRONT OR RIGHT BACK

RIGHT FRONT OR LEFT BACK

13½"

10 (10½, 10½, 10½, 11)"

9 (9, 9½, 10, 10)"

4½ (5¼, 5¼, 5½, 5½)"

9½ (10, 10¾, 11¾, 12½)"

11 (11¾, 12½. 13¼, 14)"

↑ = **Direction of work**

Collar

With 24"/60cm circular needle and 1 strand A and B held tog, pick up and k 64 (68, 68, 72, 72) sts evenly spaced around neck edge. Join and pm for beg of rnd. Work in rnds of k2, p2 rib for 5"/12.5cm. Drop A and p 8 rnds with B only. Bind off loosely. Thread tie through all 4 openings and tie at front (see photo). ■

Oversized T-Shirt

Part tee, part poncho, Rosemary Drysdale's oversized turtleneck uses texture to play up the topper's contrasting colorblocks. Ribbed sleeves and a cowl neck complete the look.

SIZES

Sized for Small/Medium, Large/X-Large and shown in size Small/Medium.

KNITTED MEASUREMENTS

Bust 49 (55)"/124.5 (139.5)cm
Length 23 (24)"/58.5 (61)cm

MATERIALS

• 4 (5) 1¾oz/50g balls (each approx 122yd/113m) of Tahki Yarns/Tahki•Stacy Charles *Tara Tweed* (wool/nylon) each in #002 fog tweed (MC) and #015 teal tweed (B) (4)

• 2 (3) balls in #018 lilac tweed (A)

• One pair size 7 (4.5mm) needles OR SIZE TO OBTAIN GAUGE

• One pair size 8 (5mm) needles

• Size 8 (5mm) circular needle, 16"/40cm long

• Stitch markers and stitch holders

GAUGE

17 sts and 23 rows = 4"/10cm over St st using smaller needles.
TAKE TIME TO CHECK GAUGE.

SEED STITCH

(over an odd number of sts)
Row 1 K1, *p1, k1; rep from * to end.
Row 2 K the purl sts and p the knit sts.
Rep row 2 for seed st.

BACK

With smaller needles and A, cast on 105 (117) sts. Cut A.
Row 1 (WS) With B, purl.
With B, work in seed st until piece measures 4½"/11.5cm from beg, end with a WS row. Cut B.
Next row (RS) With A, knit.
With A, work in seed st until piece measures 8"/20.5cm from beg. Cut A.
Change to MC and work in St st (k on RS, p on WS) until piece measures 23 (24)"/58.5 (61)cm from beg, end with a WS row.
Bind off 33 (38) sts at beg of next 2 rows. Place rem 39 (41) sts on a holder for back neck.

FRONT

Work as for back until piece measures 22 (23)"/56 (58.5)cm from beg, end with a WS row.

Neck shaping

Next row (RS) K37 (42), place center 31 (33) sts on a holder for front neck, join 2nd ball of yarn and k to end. Working both sides at once, bind off 2 sts from each neck edge twice—33 (38) sts rem each

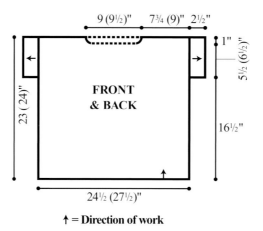

9 (9½)" 7¾ (9)" 2½"

23 (24)"

1"

5½ (6½)"

FRONT & BACK

16½"

24½ (27½)"

↑ = **Direction of work**

side. Work even until piece measures same as back to shoulders. Bind off.

FINISHING

Block pieces lightly to measurements. Sew shoulder seams. Place markers (pm) 6½ (7½)"/16.5 (19)cm from shoulder seam on front and back edges for sleeves.

Sleeves

With RS facing, larger needles and B, pick up 62 (70) sts between sleeve markers.

Row 1 (WS) P2, *k2, p2; rep from * to end.

Cont in k2, p2 rib until sleeve measures 2½"/6.5cm, end with a RS row. Cut B.

Next row (WS) With A, purl.

Bind off loosely in rib.

Sew side and sleeve seams.

Cowl neck

With RS facing, circular needle and B, beg at left shoulder seam, pick up and k 13 sts along left front

neck, k31 (33) from front neck holder, pick up and k 13 sts along right front neck, k39 (41) from back neck holder—96 (100) sts. Join and pm for beg of rnd.

Next rnd *K2, p2, rep from * around for k2, p2 rib. Cont in rib until neck measures 10"/25.5cm. Cut B.

Next rnd With A, purl. With A, bind off loosely in rib. ■

Tapered Pullover

Renée Lorion gets right into the swing of things with a lace-edged sweater with bell sleeves. The pullover is tapered just so by changing needle size.

SIZES

Sized for Small, Medium, Large, X-Large, XX-Large and shown in size Medium.

KNITTED MEASUREMENTS

Bust 36 (40, 44, 48, 52)"/91.5 (101.5, 111.5, 122, 132)cm

Length 24½ (25½, 26, 27, 27½)"/62 (65, 66, 68.5, 70)cm

Upper arm 14½ (15¼, 15¾, 16, 16½)"/37 (38.5, 40, 40.5, 42)cm

MATERIALS

• 4 (4, 5, 5, 6) 3½oz/100g hanks (each approx 218yd/200m) of AslanTrends *Artesanal* (cotton/alpaca/polyamide) in 180 raffia (**4**)

• One pair each sizes 8, 9, 10, 11, 13, and 15 (5, 5.5, 6, 8, 9, and 10mm) needles, OR SIZE TO OBTAIN GAUGES

• Size 8 (5mm) circular needle, 24"/60cm long

• Stitch holder

GAUGES

16 sts and 22 rows = 4"/10cm over St st using size 8 (5mm) needles.

14.5 sts and 20 rows = 4"/10cm over St st using size 9 (5.5mm) needles.

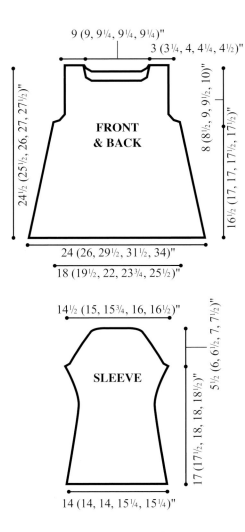

9 (9, 9¼, 9¼, 9¼)"

3 (3¼, 4, 4¼, 4½)"

FRONT & BACK

24½ (25½, 26, 27, 27½)"

8 (8½, 9, 9½, 10)"

16½ (17, 17, 17½, 17½)"

24 (26, 29½, 31½, 34)"

18 (19½, 22, 23¾, 25½)"

14½ (15, 15¾, 16, 16½)"

SLEEVE

5½ (6, 6½, 7, 7½)"

17 (17½, 18, 18, 18½)"

14 (14, 14, 15¼, 15¼)"

11 sts and 14 rows = 4"/10cm over St st using size 15 (10mm) needles.

TAKE TIME TO CHECK GAUGES.

LACE MESH

(multiple of 3 sts)

Row 1 (RS) K2, *yo, sl 1, k2, pass slipped st over each of the 2 sts just knit; rep from *, end k1.

Rows 2 and 4 Purl.

Row 3 K1, *Sl 1, k2, pass slipped st over each of the 2 sts just knit, yo; rep from *, end k2.

BACK

With size 15 (10mm) needles, cast on 66 (72, 81, 87, 93) sts. Work rows 1–4 of lace mesh. Work in St st for 12 rows. Change to size 13 (9mm) needles and cont in St st for 12 rows. Change to size 11 (8mm) needles and cont in St st for 14 rows. Change to size 10 (6mm) needles and cont in St st for 14 rows. Change to size 9 (5.5mm) and cont in St st until piece measures 16½ (17, 17, 17½, 17½)"/42 (43, 43, 44.5, 44.5)cm from beg.

Armhole shaping

Change to size 8 (5mm) needles. Bind off 2 sts at beg of next 2 (4, 4, 6, 6) rows, then 1 st at beg of next 2 (2, 4, 4, 8) rows—60 (62, 69, 71, 73) sts. Work even until armhole measures 7½ (8, 8½, 9, 9½)"/19 (20.5, 21.5, 23, 24)cm.

Neck shaping

Next row (RS) K17 (18, 21, 22, 23), sl center 26 (26, 27, 27, 27) sts to a holder for neck, join another strand of yarn and work rem 17 (18, 21, 22, 23) sts. Working both sides at once, dec 1 st at each neck edge every row 5 times. Bind off rem 12 (13, 16, 17, 18) sts.

FRONT

Work as for back until armhole measures 6¼ (6¾, 7¼, 7¾, 8¼)"/16 (17, 18.5, 19.5, 21)cm.

Neck shaping

Next row (RS) K17 (18, 21, 22, 23), sl center 26 (26, 27, 27, 27) sts to a holder for neck, join another strand of yarn and work rem 17 (18, 21, 22, 23) sts. Working both sides at once, dec 1 st at each neck edge every other row 5 times. Bind off rem 12 (13, 16, 17, 18) sts.

SLEEVES

With size 15 (10mm) needles, cast on 39 (39, 39, 42, 42) sts. Work rows 1–4 of lace mesh. Work in St st for 12 rows. Change to size 13 (9mm) needles and cont in St st for 12 rows. Change to size 11 (8mm) needles and cont in St st for 14 rows. Change to size 10 (6mm) needles, inc 1 st each side every 4th row 4 times. Work until piece measures 13 (13½, 13½, 13¾, 13¾)"/33 (34, 34, 35, 35)cm from beg. Change to size 9 (5.5mm) needles, inc 1 st each side every 4th row 3 (4, 5, 4, 5) times—53 (55, 57, 58, 60) sts. Work even until piece measures 17 (17½, 17½, 18, 18)"/43 (44.5, 44.5, 45.5, 45.5)cm from beg.

Cap shaping

Change to size 8 (5mm) needles and bind off 2 sts at beg of next 2 (4, 4, 6, 8) rows. Dec 1 st each side every other row 12 (12, 14, 10, 7) times, every 4th

row 0 (0, 0, 2, 4) times. Bind off 3 (2, 2, 2, 2) sts at beg of next 2 rows, 3 (3, 2, 2, 2) sts at beg of next 2 rows. Bind off rem 13 (13, 13, 14, 14) sts.

FINISHING

Sew shoulder seams.

Neckband

With circular needle, pick up and k 6 (6, 7, 7, 7) sts along back right neck edge, k 26 (26, 27, 27, 27) sts from holder, pick up and k 13 sts along back left neck edge and front left neck, k 26 (26, 27, 27, 27) sts from front holder, pick up and k 7 sts along front right neck—78 (78, 81, 81, 81) sts. Join, k one round. Work rows 1–3 of lace mesh. Bind off. Sew side and sleeve seams. ■

Side Button Poncho

Amanda Keep's geometrically colorblocked poncho, knit intarsia-style in stockinette, buttons up the side to stay securely in place.

SIZES

Sized for Small/Medium, Large/X-Large/XX-Large and shown in size Small/Medium.

KNITTED MEASUREMENTS

Width 51"/129.5cm
Length 21 (23)"/53.5 (58.5)cm

MATERIALS

• 4 (5) .88oz/25g balls (each approx 114yd/104m) of Berroco *Cirrus* (mohair/nylon/wool) each in #2511 gulf of mexico (teal A) and #2516 punaluu beach (black C) **[5]**

• 2 balls each in #2509 erie sunset (rose B) and #2512 sequoia (dark green D)

• Size 10 (6mm) circular needles, one each 16"/40cm and 47"/120cm long, OR SIZE TO OBTAIN GAUGE

• Six 1"/25mm buttons

• Stitch marker

GAUGE

14 sts and 22 rows = 4"/10cm over St st using size 10 (6mm) needles.
TAKE TIME TO CHECK GAUGE.

NOTES

1) Poncho is knit in one piece beg at lower front edge.

2) When changing colors, twist yarns on WS to prevent holes in work.

3) Longer circular needle is used to accommodate large number of sts. Do not join.

PONCHO

With longer circular needle and A, cast on 105 sts, with B, cast on 11 sts, with C, cast on 60 sts—176 sts.

Next row (RS) With C, k60, with B, k11, with A, k105.

Working in St st (k on RS, p on WS), cont in pat as established until piece measures 12 (14)"/30.5 (35.5)cm from beg, end with a WS row. Cut A.

Next row (RS) With C, k60, with B, k to end.

Cont in pat as established until piece measures 15 (17)"/38 (43)cm from beg, end with a WS row. Cut B.

Next row (RS) With C, knit.

Cont with C only until piece measures 18 (20)"/45.5 (51)cm from beg, end with a WS row. Cut C.

Next row (RS) With D, k45, with A, k to end.

Cont in pat as established until piece measures 19 (21)"/48 (53.5)cm from beg, end with a WS row. Cut A.

Next row (RS) With D, knit.

Cont with D only until piece measures 21 (23)"/53.5 (58.5)cm from beg, end with a WS row.

Neck shaping

Next row (RS) K67, bind off 42 sts, k to end.

Next row (WS) P67, cast on 42 sts, place marker (pm) for neck edge, p to end.

Cont with D only until piece measures 2"/5cm from neck marker, end with a RS row.

Note Color changes will now take place on WS rows.

Next row (WS) With D, p45, with A, p to end.

Cont in pat until piece measures 3"/7.5cm from neck marker, end with a RS row. Cut D and A.

Next row (WS) With C, purl.

Cont with C only until piece measures 6"/15cm from neck marker, end with a RS row.

Next row (WS) With C, p60, with B, p to end.

Cont in pat until piece measures 9"/23cm from neck marker, end with a RS row.

Next row (WS) With C, p60, with B, p11, with A, p to end.

Cont in pat until piece measures 21 (23)"/53.5 (58.5)cm from neck marker.

Note Changing colors 1 st before color block begins in bind-off row will keep bound-off sts in pat.

Bind-off row (RS) With A, bind off 104 sts, with B, bind off 11 sts, with C, bind off rem sts.

FINISHING

Fold poncho at neck so lower edges align. Sew 3 buttons 1"/2.5cm from each front side edge through both layers of fabric, the first 2"/5cm from lower edge, the 2nd 7"/18cm from lower edge, and the 3rd placed between.

Collar

With shorter circular needle and B, pick up and k 82 sts evenly around neck edge. Join and pm for beg of rnd. Work in St st (k every rnd) until collar measures 1"/2.5cm. Bind off loosely. ∎

Mitered Cardi

Mari Lynn Patrick's snowy-white cropped cardi is knit in two pieces from center to sleeve edge, then seamed up the back. Mitered corners complete the sides.

SIZE

Sized for Small, Medium, Large, X-Large, XX-Large and shown in size Small.

KNITTED MEASUREMENTS

Lower edge 40 (42, 44, 46, 48)"/101.5 (106.5, 111.5, 117, 122)cm

Bust 34 (36, 38, 40, 42)"/86 (91.5, 96.5, 101.5, 106.5)cm

Length 20 (21, 22, 23, 24)"/51 (53, 56, 58.5, 61)cm

Upper arm 14 (15, 15, 16, 17)"/35.5 (38, 38, 40.5, 43)cm

MATERIALS

• 8 (9, 10, 11, 12) 3½oz/100g hanks (each approx 45yd/41m) of *Blue Sky Alpacas* (alpaca/wool) in #1004 polar bear 🔵❻

• Size 15 (10mm) circular needle, 24"/60cm long, OR SIZE TO OBTAIN GAUGES

• Size J-10 (6mm) crochet hook

• Stitch markers

GAUGES

8 sts and 16 rows = 4"/10cm over garter st using size 15 (10mm) needle.

8 sts and 10 rows = 4"/10cm over St st using size 15 (10mm) needle.

TAKE TIME TO CHECK GAUGES.

NOTE

Cardigan is constructed in 2 pieces, the left half and the right half. Each piece begins by casting on at the center back/lower/center front edge and ends at the sleeve cuff. The 2 pieces are then seamed up the center back. This garment is close-fitting due to the bulk of the yarn.

LEFT SIDE

Beg at the center back/lower/center left front edge, cast on 112 (118, 124, 130, 136) sts.

Row 1 (RS) K42 (44, 46, 48, 50) for center back, pm; k42 (44, 46, 48, 50) for lower edge, pm; k28 (30, 32, 34, 36) for center left front.

Row 2 (WS) K1, k1 into front and back of next st (for neck inc), *k to 2 sts before marker, ssk, sl marker, k2tog; rep from * once more, k to end.

Row 3 (RS) K to the last 2 sts, k1 into front and back of next st (for neck inc), k1.

Row 4-15 Rep the last 2 rows 6 times more. There are 35 (37, 39, 41, 43) sts before first marker (for center back); 28 (30, 32, 34, 36) sts between first and 2nd marker (for lower edge); 35 (37, 39, 41, 43) sts after 2nd marker (for center left front). This is the end of the back neck and center neck shaping.

Shoulder shaping

Row 16 (WS) *K to 2 sts before marker, ssk, sl marker, k2tog; rep from * once more, k to end.

Row 17 K to first marker, sl marker, k0 (1, 2, 3, 4), [k4, k2tog, k2] 3 times, k2 (3, 4, 5, 6), sl marker, k to end. There are 23 (25, 27, 29, 31) sts between markers.

Row 18 Rep row 16.

Stockinette stitch segment

Row 19 (RS) K2, k2tog (for shoulder dec), *k to 2 sts before marker, ssk, sl marker, k2tog; rep from * once, k to last 4 sts, ssk, k2.

Row 20 (WS) *Purl to 2 sts before marker, p2tog, sl marker, p2tog tbl; rep from * once, purl to end.

Row 21 *K to 2 sts before marker, ssk, sl marker, k2tog; rep from * once more, k to end.

Row 22 Rep row 20.

Rows 23–26 Rep rows 19–22.

Row 27 Rep row 19.

For size Medium only

Row 28 Purl.

Row 29 Rep row 21.

For size Large only

Row 28 Purl.

Row 29 Rep row 21.

Row 30 Purl.

Row 31 Rep row 19.

For size X-Large only

Row 28 Purl.

Row 29 Rep row 21.

Row 30 Purl.

Row 31 Rep row 19.

Row 32 Purl.

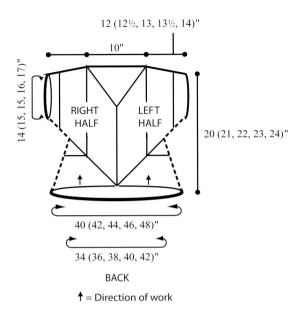

12 (12½, 13, 13½, 14)"

10"

14 (15, 15, 16, 17)"

RIGHT HALF   LEFT HALF

20 (21, 22, 23, 24)"

40 (42, 44, 46, 48)"

34 (36, 38, 40, 42)"

BACK

↑ = Direction of work

Row 33 Rep row 21.

For size XX-Large only

Row 28 Purl.

Row 29 Rep row 21.

Row 30 Purl.

Row 31 Rep row 21.

Row 32 Purl.

Row 33 Rep row 21.

Row 34 Purl.

Row 35 Rep row 19.

For all sizes

Row 28 (30, 32, 34, 36) (WS) P to 2 sts before first marker, p2tog, remove first marker, p3tog, slip (but do not remove) 2nd marker, p2tog tbl, p to end. There are 41 (43, 43, 45, 47) sts.

Begin sleeve

Row 29 (31, 33, 35, 37) (RS) K2, k2tog, k to 2 sts before marker, ssk, sl marker, k1, k2tog, k to last 4 sts, ssk, k2.

Row 30 (32, 34, 36, 38) Purl.

Row 31 (33, 35, 37, 39) K2, k2tog, k to 2 sts before marker, ssk, sl marker, k1, k2tog, k to last 4 sts, ssk, k2.

Next row Purl.

Next row (RS) K2, k2tog, k to 2 sts before marker, ssk, sl marker, k1, k2tog, k to last 4 sts, ssk, k2—29 (31, 31, 33, 35) sts. Remove marker and k the last 5 rows. Bind off.

RIGHT FRONT

Beg as for the left half, cast on 112 (118, 124, 130, 136) sts.

Row 1 (RS) K28 (30, 32, 34, 36) for center right front, pm; k42 (44, 46, 48, 50) for lower edge, pm; k42 (44, 46, 48, 50) for center back.

Row 2 (WS) *K to 2 sts before marker, ssk, sl marker, k2tog; rep from * once more, k to last 2 sts, k1 into front and back of next st (for neck inc), k1.

Row 3 (RS) K1, k1 into front and back of next st, k to end.

Rows 4–15 Rep the last 2 rows (rows 2 and 3) 6 times more. There are 35 (37, 39, 41, 43) sts before first marker (for center front); 28 (30, 32, 34, 36) sts between first and 2nd markers (for lower edge); 35 (37, 39, 41, 43) sts after 2nd marker (for center back). This is the end of the back neck and center front neck shaping.

Shoulder shaping

Beg at row 16 of the left half, work same as for left half through to the end of the piece and bind off final 29 (31, 31, 33, 35) sts for sleeve.

FINISHING

Do not block pieces. Using crochet hook and working from the WS, loosely sl st the center back seam tog so that cast-on ridge shows along both edges. Sew the shoulder seams.

Collar

Pick up and k 15 sts from shaped right front neck, 17 sts from back neck edge, 15 sts from shaped left front—47 sts.

Row 1 (WS) K3, k2tog, k to last 5 sts, ssk, k3.

Rows 2–4 Rep row 1—39 sts. Bind off. ■

Drop-Shoulder Top

Unusual detailing—including diagonal shaping that wraps from back to front with pretty increases and decreases—raises the profile of Rosemary Drysdale's relaxed-fit, drop-shoulder pullover.

SIZES

Sized for Small, Medium, Large, X-Large, 2X, 3X and shown in size Medium.

KNITTED MEASUREMENTS

Bust 43 (45½, 49, 52, 55, 58)"/109 (115.5, 124.5, 132, 139.5, 147)cm

Length 18½ (19, 20, 20½, 21½, 22)"/47 (48, 51, 52, 54.5, 56)cm

Upper arm 13 (14, 14¾, 16, 17, 18)"/33 (35.5, 37.5, 40.5, 43, 45.5)cm

MATERIALS

• 9 (9, 10, 11, 12, 13) 2oz/57g hanks (each approx 120yd/110m) of Prism Yarns *Tencel Tape* (tencel) in #301 light blue ❸

• One pair size 10½ (6.5mm) needles, OR SIZE TO OBTAIN GAUGE

• One size 10½ (6.5mm) circular needle, 16"/40cm long, for collar

• Stitch holders

• Stitch markers

GAUGE

18 sts and 24 rows = 4"/10cm over St st using size 10½ (6.5mm) needles.
TAKE TIME TO CHECK GAUGE.

K1, P1 RIB

(over an odd number of sts)

Row 1 *K1, p1; rep from *, end k1.

Row 2 K the knit sts and p the purl sts.

Rep row 2 for k1, p1 rib.

BACK

Cast on 131 (137, 145, 151, 159, 165) sts. Work in k1, p1 rib for 2"/5cm.

Beg shaping detail

Next (dec) row (RS) K2, k2tog, k to last 4 sts, k2tog tbl, k2—129 (135, 143, 149, 157, 163) sts.

Next row Purl.

Rep last 2 rows 16 times more—97 (103, 111, 117, 125, 131) sts.

Cont in St st (k on RS, p on WS) and work even until piece measures 17¾ (18¼, 19¼, 19¾, 20¾, 21¼)"/45 (46.5, 49, 50, 52.5, 54)cm from beg, end with a WS row.

Neck and shoulder shaping

Next row (RS) K31 (33, 35, 38, 41, 44), place next 35 (37, 41, 41, 43, 43) sts on holder, join 2nd ball of yarn, k to end. Working both sides at once, cont on 31 (33, 35, 38, 41, 44) sts each side for 4 more rows. Place sts on holders.

FRONT

Cast on 63 (69, 77, 83, 91, 97) sts. Work in k1, p1 rib for 2"/5cm.

Beg shaping detail

Next (inc) row (RS) K3, M1, k to last 3 sts, M1, k3— 65 (71, 79, 85, 93, 99) sts.

Next row Purl.

Rep last 2 rows 16 times more—97 (103, 111, 117, 125, 131) sts.

Work even in St st until piece measures 15½ (16, 17, 17½, 18½, 19)"/39.5 (40.5, 43, 44.5, 47, 48)cm from beg, end with a WS row.

Neck shaping

Next row (RS) K41 (43, 45, 48, 51, 54), place center 15 (17, 21, 21, 23, 23) sts on a holder, join 2nd ball of yarn, k to end.

Working both sides at once, bind off 2 sts from each neck edge 4 times, then dec 1 st at each neck edge every other row twice. Work even on rem 31 (33, 35, 38, 41, 44) sts each side until front measures same as back. Place sts on holders.

SLEEVES

Cast on 40 (42, 46, 46, 48, 50) sts. Work in k1, p1 rib as foll:

Row 1 *K1, p1; rep from * to end.

Row 2 K the knit sts and p the purl sts. Rep row 2 until piece measures 2"/5cm from beg. Work 6 rows in St st.

Next (inc) row (RS) K1, M1, k to last st, M1, k1—42 (44, 48, 48, 50, 52) sts. Rep inc row every 6th (6th, 6th, 4th, 4th, 4th) row 5 (9, 7, 7, 9, 15) times more, then every 8th (0, 8th, 6th, 6th, 0) row 3 (0,

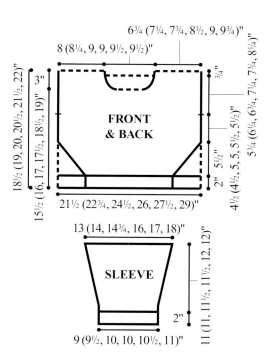

2, 5, 4, 0) times—58 (62, 66, 72, 76, 82) sts. Work even in St st until sleeve measures 13 (13, 13½, 13½, 14, 14)"/33 (33, 34.5, 34.5, 35.5, 35.5)cm from beg. Bind off loosely.

FINISHING

Join shoulders using 3-needle bind-off. Center sleeve tops to shoulder seams and sew in. Beg above rib, sew side seams to underarms. Sew sleeve seams.

Collar

With RS facing, k 35 (37, 41, 41, 43, 43) sts from back neck holder, pick up and k 23 sts along neck to front neck holder, k 15 (17, 21, 21, 23, 23) sts from front neck holder, pick up and k 23 sts for back neck, pm and join—96 (100, 108, 108, 112, 112) sts. Work in k1, p1 rib as for sleeve, until collar measures 2"/5cm. Bind off loosely. Fold collar to inside and sew down. ■

Cowl Neck Tunic

The creative colorscaping on Maie Landra's relaxed turtleneck tunic comes from working a trio of colorways two at a time.

SIZES

Sized for Small, Medium, Large, 1X, 2X and shown in size Small.

KNITTED MEASUREMENTS

Bust 40 (43, 48, 53, 55½)"/101.5 (109, 122, 134.5, 141)cm

Length 28 (28½, 29, 29½, 30)"/71 (72, 73.5, 74.5, 76)cm

MATERIALS

• 7 (8, 9, 10, 11) 1¾oz/50g hanks (each approx 114yd/100m) of Koigu Wool Designs *Kersti* (wool) each in K300 (A) and K118C (B) 🔳

• 3 hanks in K716D (C)

• One pair each sizes 10 and 10½ (6 and 6.5mm) needles OR SIZE TO OBTAIN GAUGE

• Size 10 (6mm) circular needle, 24"/60cm long

• Stitch markers

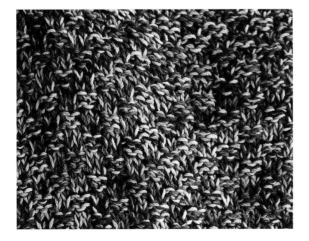

GAUGE

13 sts and 20 rows = 4"/10cm over double moss st with 1 strand each of A and B held tog using larger needles.

TAKE TIME TO CHECK GAUGE.

DOUBLE MOSS STITCH

(multiple of 4 sts plus 2)

Row 1 (RS) *K2, p2; rep from *, end k2.

Rows 2 and 4 K the knit sts and p the purl sts.

Row 3 *P2, k2; rep from *, end p2.

Rep rows 1–4 for double moss st.

K1, P2 RIB

Row 1 (RS) *K1, p2; rep from * to end.

Row 2 K the knit sts and p the purl sts. Rep row 2 for k1, p2 rib.

BACK

With smaller needles and 1 strand each of A and B held tog, cast on 60 (63, 72, 81, 84) sts. Work in k1, p2 rib for 4 rows, inc 6 (7, 6, 5, 6) sts evenly across last WS row—66 (70, 78, 86, 90) sts. Change to larger needles. Work in double moss st until piece measures 19"/48cm from beg, end with a WS row.

Sleeve shaping

Note Work inc'd sts into double moss st.

Cast on 3 sts at beg of next 2 rows—72 (76, 84, 92,

96) sts. Place markers at each end of last row. Inc 1 st each side on next row, then every other row 8 (8, 6, 5, 5) times more—90 (94, 98, 104, 108) sts. Cont in pat until sleeve measures 8 (8½, 9, 9½, 10)"/20.5 (21.5, 23, 24, 25.5)cm from marked row, end with a WS row.

Neck shaping

Next row (RS) Work 30 (32, 34, 36, 38) sts, join a 2nd ball each of A and B, bind off center 30 (30, 30, 32, 32) sts, work to end. Work both sides at once until sleeve measures 1"/2.5cm from center bind-off. Bind off sts each side for shoulders.

FRONT

Work as for back until sleeve measures 6 (6½, 7, 7½, 8)"/15.5 (16.5, 18, 19, 20.5)cm from markers. Shape neck as for back. Cont on rem 30 (32, 34, 36, 38) each side until sleeve measures same as back. Bind off sts each side for shoulders.

FINISHING

Sew shoulder seams.

Cowl

With RS facing, circular needle and 1 strand each of A and C held tog, pick up and k 84 (84, 84, 88, 88) sts evenly around front and back neck edge. Join and work in k1, p1 rib for 8 rnds.
Next (inc) rnd [K1, p1, k1 into same st, rib 7 sts] 9 times, [k1, p1, k1 into same st, rib 5 (5, 5, 7, 7) sts] 2 times—106 (106, 106, 110, 110) sts. Cont in rib until cowl measures 13½"/34.5cm. Bind off loosely in rib.

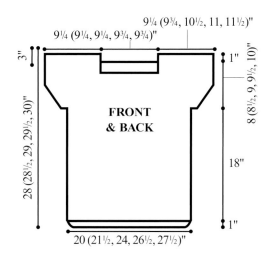

9¼ (9¾, 10½, 11, 11½)"
9¼ (9¼, 9¼, 9¾, 9¾)"
3"
1"
8 (8½, 9, 9½, 10)"

FRONT & BACK

28 (28½, 29, 29½, 30)"
18"
1"
20 (21½, 24, 26½, 27½)"

Sleeve trim

With larger needles and 1 strand each of A and C held tog, pick up and k 50 (52, 4, 56, 58) sts evenly between front and back markers. Work 6 rows in k1, p1 rib. Bind off loosely in rib.

Pocket placement

Place markers for pockets at 7"/18cm and 12"/30.5cm up from lower edge on each side. Sew side seams, including cast-on sleeve sts and side of sleeve trim, leaving space between pocket markers open.

Pocket trim

With larger needle and 1 strand each of A and B held tog, pick up and k 18 sts along front edge of pocket opening. Work 6 rows in k1, p1 rib. Bind off in rib.

Pocket linings

With RS facing, smaller needles and 1 strand of any color, pick up and k 20 sts along inside front pocket edge. Work in St st for 4"/10cm. Bind off. Rep for inside back pocket edge. Sew 3 sides of pocket linings tog. ■

Tie Tunic

Rosemary Drysdale draws attention to a modern silhouette by bordering her sloped-shoulder tunic with wide ribbing and cinching it with a dramatic drawstring-style belt.

SIZES

Sized for Small, Medium, Large, X-Large, XX-Large and shown in size Small.

KNITTED MEASUREMENTS

Bust 46½ (48½, 50½, 52½, 54½)"/118 (123, 128, 133, 138.5)cm

Length 34 (35, 36, 37, 38)"/86.5 (89, 91.5, 94, 96.5)cm

MATERIALS

• 14 (16, 17, 18, 19) 1¾oz/50g balls (each approx 84yd/77m) Tahki Yarns/Tahki•Stacy Charles, Inc. *Juno* (alpaca/nylon) in #05 charcoal (**5**) *

• One pair each sizes 9 and 10 (5.5 and 6mm) needles OR SIZE TO OBTAIN GAUGE

• One size 10 (6mm) circular needle, 24"/60cm long

• Stitch markers

GAUGE

16 sts and 22 rows = 4"/10cm over St st using smaller needles.
TAKE TIME TO CHECK GAUGE.

BACK

With larger needles, cast on 93 (97, 102, 107, 112) sts.

Beg rib pat

Row 1 (RS) P0 (2, 2, 2, 2), *k3, p2; rep from *, end k3 (0, 0, 0, 0).

Row 2 P3 (0, 0, 0, 0), *k2, p3; rep from *, end k0 (2, 2, 2, 2). Rep rows 1 and 2 until rib measures 5"/12.5cm, dec 0 (0, 1, 2, 3) sts on last (WS) row—93 (97, 101, 105, 109) sts. Change to smaller needles. Work in St st until piece measures 18 (19, 20, 20, 20)"/45.5 (48, 51, 51, 51)cm from beg, end with a WS row.

Divide for belt slits

Next row (RS) K30 (32, 34, 36, 38), join 2nd ball of yarn and k33, join 3rd ball of yarn and k30 (32, 34, 36, 38). Working all 3 sections at once, work 11 rows even. Cut 2nd and 3rd balls of yarn.

Joining row (RS) Cont working with original yarn, and k across all 93 (97, 101, 105, 109) sts. Work even until piece measures 28 (29, 30, 31, 32)"/71 (73.5, 76, 78.5, 81)cm from beg, end with a WS row.

Shoulder shaping

Dec row (RS) K2tog, k to last 2 sts, ssk. Rep dec row

* Yarn used in original pattern is no longer available and is listed on page 190.

DRAMATIC SHAPES

every other row 13 times more—65 (69, 73, 77, 81) sts. Work 1 row even. Bind off 6 (6, 8, 8, 8) sts at beg of next 2 rows, 6 (7, 7, 7, 8) sts at beg of next 4 rows. Bind off rem 29 (29, 29, 33, 33) sts.

FRONT

Work as for back until piece measures 26 (27, 28, 29, 30)"/66 (68.5, 71, 73.5, 76)cm from beg.

V-neck shaping

Next row (RS) K46 (48, 50, 52, 54), join 2nd ball of yarn and bind off 1 st, k to end—46 (48, 50, 52, 54) sts each side. Working both sides at once, dec 1 st at each neck edge every RS row 14 (14, 14, 16, 16) times, AT SAME TIME, when piece measures same length as back to shoulder shaping, shape shoulders as for back.

FINISHING

Block pieces to measurements. Sew shoulder seams.

Neckband

With RS facing and circular needle, beg at center front neck and pick up and k 98 (98, 98, 103, 103) sts evenly around neck edge. Work back and forth in rib pat as foll:
Row 1 (WS) *P3, k2; rep from *, end p3.
Row 2 *K3, p2; rep from *, end k3. Rep last 2 rows 3 times more. Bind off in rib pat. Sew ends of band to edges of center front neck, overlapping left front band over right.

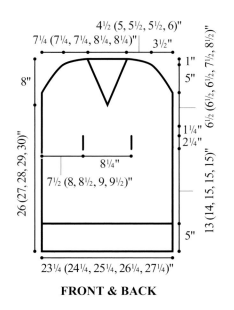

4½ (5, 5½, 5½, 6)"
7¼ (7¼, 7¼, 8¼, 8¼)"
3½"
1"
5"
8"
6½ (6½, 6½, 7½, 8½)"
1¼"
2¼"
26 (27, 28, 29, 30)"
8¼"
7½ (8, 8½, 9, 9½)"
13 (14, 15, 15, 15)"
5"
23¼ (24¼, 25¼, 26¼, 27¼)"

FRONT & BACK

Armhole bands

Place a marker on each side edge of front and back, 6½ (6½, 6½, 7½, 8½)"/16.5 (16.5, 16.5, 16.5, 19, 21.5)cm down from shoulder. With RS facing and larger needles, pick up and k 48 (48, 48, 53, 63) sts evenly between front and back markers. Work same as for neckband.
Sew side seams, including armhole bands.

Belt

With smaller needles, cast on 18 sts.
Row 1 (RS) *K3, p2; rep from * end, k3. Cont to work in k3, p2 rib for 53 (57, 61, 63, 65)"/134.5 (145, 155, 160, 165)cm, or desired length. Bind off in rib.
Thread one end of belt through first slit from front to back, across inside back and through 2nd slit from back to front. ■

Cowl Neck Dress

Annabelle Speer's mod dress gets its silhouette cues from its dropped, sloped shoulders and cowl collar.

SIZES

Sized for Small, Medium, Large, X-Large, XX-Large and shown in size Small.

KNITTED MEASUREMENTS

Bust 42 (44, 46, 50, 52)"/106.5 (111.5, 117, 127, 132)cm

Length 33 (33, 34, 35, 35)"/84 (84, 86.5, 89, 89)cm

MATERIALS

- 15 (16, 17, 19, 20) 1¾oz/50g hanks (each approx 86yd/75m) of Be Sweet Simply Sweet *Whipped Cream* (kid mohair/wool/silk) in #804 grape ④

- Size 8 (5mm) needles OR SIZE TO OBTAIN GAUGE

- One each sizes 8 and 9 (5mm and 5.5mm) circular needles, each 16"/40cm long

- Stitch markers and stitch holder

GAUGE

19 sts and 22 rows = 4"/10cm over rib pat using size 8 (5mm) needles.

TAKE TIME TO CHECK GAUGE.

BROKEN RIB

(over an odd number of sts)

Row 1 (RS) K1, *p1, k1; rep from * to end.

Row 2 (WS) Purl.

Rep rows 1 and 2 for broken rib.

BACK

With straight needles, cast on 93 (99, 103, 113, 117) sts. Work in broken rib until piece measures 4"/10cm from beg.

Next (inc) row (RS) K1, M1, work to last st, M1, k1— 95 (101, 105, 115, 119) sts. Cont in pat as established, rep inc row every 4"/10cm twice

more—99 (105, 109, 119, 123) sts.

Work even until piece measures 27 (27, 28, 29, 29)"/68.5 (68.5, 71, 73.5, 73.5)cm from beg.

Shoulder shaping

Note Place marker (pm) at beg and end of last row for shoulder shaping. Do not slip these markers.

Dec row (RS) K2tog, work to last 2 sts, ssk. Rep dec row every other row 12 times more—73 (79, 83, 93, 97) sts. Work 1 WS row even in pat.

Bind off 8 (8, 10, 10, 10) sts at beg of next 2 rows, 7 (8, 8, 9, 10) sts at beg of next 4 rows. Leave rem 29 (31, 31, 37, 37) sts on holder for back neck.

FRONT

Work same as for back until piece measures 2"/5cm from shoulder marker.

Neck shaping

Next row (RS) Cont shoulder shaping, work pat to center 19 (21, 21, 23, 23) sts, place center sts on a holder, join 2nd ball of yarn and work to end. Working both sides at once, bind off 3 (3, 3, 4, 4) sts from each neck edge once, 2 (2, 2, 3, 3) sts once, AT SAME TIME, cont to shape shoulders as for back.

FINISHING

Sew shoulder seams from neck edge to marker. Place a marker on each side edge of front and back 7 (7½, 8, 8, 8½)"/18 (19, 20.5, 20.5, 21.5)cm down from shoulder marker for armhole. Sew side seams from lower edges to armhole markers.

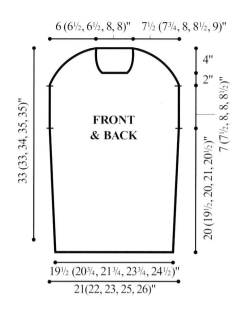

6 (6½, 6½, 8, 8)"   7½ (7¾, 8, 8½, 9)"

4"

2"

FRONT & BACK

33 (33, 34, 35, 35)"

7 (7½, 8, 8, 8½)"

20 (19½, 20, 21, 20½)"

19½ (20¾, 21¾, 23¾, 24½)"

21(22, 23, 25, 26)"

Collar

With smaller circular needle, work 29 (31, 31, 37, 37) sts from back neck holder in pat as established, pick up and k 28 sts along left front neck edge, work 19 (21, 21, 23, 23) sts from front neck holder in pat as established, pick up and k 28 sts along right front neck edge—104 (108, 108, 116, 116) sts. Join and place marker for beg of rnd.

Rnd 1 Knit.

Rnd 2 Cont in broken rib as established over all sts. Rep these two rnds until collar measures 1¾"/4.5cm, end with a rnd 2.

Next rnd Purl.

Next rnd Cont in broken rib as established. Rep these two rnds until collar measures 6¾"/17cm. Change to larger circular needle, and work until collar measures 12"/30.5cm. Bind off loosely in rib. ▨

Collared Cardi

With its generous collar, sloped shoulders and subtle color variegation, Faith Hale's broken-rib jacket is a chic layering piece that will take you from workday to evening play.

SIZES

Sized for Small, Medium, Large and shown in size Small.

KNITTED MEASUREMENTS

Bust (closed) 38 (42, 46)"/96.5 (106.5, 116.5)cm
Length 19¼ (19¾, 20¼)"/49 (50, 51.5)cm

MATERIALS

• 6 (7, 8) .88oz/25g balls (each approx 230yd/210m) of Trendsetter Yarns *Kid Seta* (mohair/silk) in #1024 brown (A) **1**

• 7 (8, 9) 1¾oz/50g balls (each approx 100yd/91m) of Trendsetter Yarns *Tonalita* (wool/acrylic) in #3117 violet eyes (multi B) **4** *

• One pair size 11 (8mm) needles OR SIZE TO OBTAIN GAUGE

• Size 11 (8mm) circular needle, 36"/90cm long

GAUGE

14 sts and 18 rows = 4"/10cm over broken rib pat using size 11 (8mm) needles with 2 strands of A and 1 strand of B held tog.
TAKE TIME TO CHECK GAUGE.

BROKEN RIB PATTERN

(multiple of 3 sts plus 2)
Rows 1 and 3 (RS) *K2, p1; rep from *, end k2.
Row 2 *P2, k1; rep from * end, p2.
Row 4 P1, k to last st, p1.
Rep rows 1–4 for broken rib pat.

K1, P1 RIB

(over an odd number of sts)
Row 1 *K1, p1; rep from *, end k1.
Row 2 *P1, k1; rep from *, end p1.
Rep rows 1 and 2 for k1, p1 rib.

NOTE

Sweater is worked with two strands of A and one strand of B held together throughout.

BACK

With straight needles, cast on 59 (65, 71) sts.
Work in broken rib pat for 16 (16½, 17)"/40.5 (42, 43)cm, end with a WS row.

Shoulder shaping

Bind off 2 (3, 3) sts at beg of next 2 (12, 6) rows.
Bind off 3 (4, 4) sts at beg of next 14 (4, 10) rows.
Bind off rem 13 sts.

* Yarn used in original pattern is no longer available and is listed on page 190.

LEFT FRONT

With straight needles, cast on 23 (26, 29) sts. Work in broken rib pat for 16 (16½, 17)"/40.5 (42, 43)cm, end with a WS row.

Shoulder shaping

Shape shoulder at beg of RS rows as for back.

RIGHT FRONT

Work to correspond to left front, reversing shaping by binding off for shoulders at beg of WS rows.

FINISHING

Sew shoulder seams.

Armhole trim

Place markers for armholes 7 (7½, 8)"/17.5 (19, 20.5)cm down from shoulder seams on fronts and back.

With straight needles and RS facing, pick up and k 55 (59, 63) sts evenly between markers. Work in

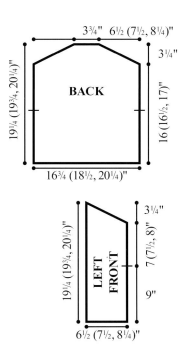

k1, p1 rib for 7 rows. Bind off. Sew side seams, including armhole trim.

Collar and front bands

With circular needle and RS facing, beg at lower edge, pick up and k 75 (77, 79) sts along right front edge, place marker (pm), pick up and k 15 sts along back neck, pm, pick up and k 75 (77, 79) sts along left front edge—165 (169, 173) sts.

Next (inc) row (WS) Beg with p1, work in k1, p1 rib to marker, slip marker (sm), [k1, p1 into next st] 15 times, sm, beg with k1, rib to end—180 (184, 188) sts. Cont in k1, p1 rib for 4 rows more.

Next (inc) row (RS) Rib to marker, sm, [(k1, p1, p1) in next st, rib 13 sts] twice, (k1, p1, p1) in next st, rib to end—186 (190, 194) sts.

Work even until collar measures 8¼ (8 ½, 9¼)"/21 (21.5, 23.5)cm. Bind off loosely in rib. ■

Cropped Raglan Pullover

Lori Steinberg's lovely cropped turtleneck has great stitch definition to show off the raglan-armhole-decrease detail and the crisp rib.

SIZES

Sized for X-Small, Small, Medium, Large and shown in size Small.

KNITTED MEASUREMENTS

Bust 33 (37, 41, 45)"/83.5 (94, 104, 114)cm*
Length 14½ (15, 15¼, 16½)"/37 (38, 40, 42)cm
Upper arm 14½ (16½, 17½, 18½)"/37 (42, 44.5, 47)cm
The finished bust measurement is approx 3"/7.5cm less than measurement given on schematic, due to the pulling-in effects of the ribbing and the raglan shaping detail.

MATERIALS

• 9 (10, 11, 13) 1⅖oz/40g hanks (each approx 100yd/91m) of Berroco *Seduce* (rayon/viscose/linen/silk/nylon) in #4469 petal (**4**) *

• One pair each sizes 5 and 7 (3.75 and 4.5mm) needles OR SIZE TO OBTAIN GAUGE

• One set (5) size 7 (4.5mm) double-pointed needles (dpns)

• Stitch holders (or scrap yarn)

• Stitch markers

GAUGE

20 sts and 30 rows = 4"/10cm over St st using larger needles.
TAKE TIME TO CHECK GAUGE.

STITCH GLOSSARY

ksp K1 and slip st back to LH needle, pass next st over st just knit and slip to RH needle for a right-slanting dec.

k2sp K2tog and slip st back to LH needle, pass next st over k2tog and slip to RH needle for a right-slanting dec.

Single dec row (RS) K3, p1, ksp, k to last 6 sts, SKP, p1, k3—1 st dec'd each side.

Double dec row (RS) K3, p1, k2sp, k to last 7 sts, SK2P, p1, k3—2 sts dec'd each side.

* Yarn used in original pattern is no longer available and is listed on page 190.

BACK

With smaller needles, cast on 92 (101, 113, 122) sts.

Row 1 (WS) P1, *k2, p1; rep from *, end p1.

Row 2 K the knit sts and p the purl sts. Rep row 2 for k1, p2 ribbing until piece measures 2¼"/7cm from beg. Change to larger needles and work in St st (k on RS, p on WS) for ¼"/2cm, end with a WS row.

Raglan armhole shaping

[Work single dec row; work 1 row even] 35 (37, 36, 39) times. [Work double dec row; work 1 row even] 0 (1, 4, 4) times—22 (23, 25, 28) sts rem. Place sts on holder.

FRONT

Work same as for back.

SLEEVES

With smaller needles, cast on 74 (80, 86, 92) sts. Work ribbing same as for back for 2¼"/7cm, end with a WS row. Change to larger needles.

Next row Knit, inc 0 (3, 2, 2) sts evenly spaced across—74 (83, 88, 94) sts.

Work in St st until piece measures 8¾"/21cm from beg, end with a WS row.

Raglan armhole shaping

[Work single dec row; work 1 row even] 25 (32, 34, 37) times. [Work single dec row; work 3 rows even] 5 (3, 3, 3) times. Bind off rem 14 (13, 14, 14) sts.

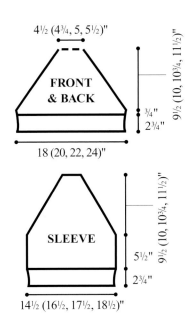

4½ (4¾, 5, 5½)"

9½ (10, 10¾, 11½)"

FRONT & BACK

¾"
2¾"

18 (20, 22, 24)"

9½ (10, 10¾, 11½)"

SLEEVE

5½"
2¾"

14½ (16½, 17½, 18½)"

FINISHING

Sew raglan sleeve caps into raglan armholes.

Turtleneck collar

Place sts from holders on dpns. Beg at left shoulder, with RS facing, pick up and k 14 (13, 14, 14) sts along top of left sleeve, k 22 (23, 25, 28) front neck sts, pick up and k 14 (13, 14, 14) sts along top of right sleeve, k 22 (23, 25, 28) back neck sts—72 (72, 78, 84) sts. Place marker for beg of rnd.

Next rnd *K2, p1; rep from * around. Rep last rnd until collar measures 8"/20.5cm from beg. Bind off sts loosely in rib.

Sew side and sleeve seams. ◼

Batwing Pullover

Only minimal finishing in necessary for Conway + Bliss's eye-catching output: the featherweight dolman-shaped pullover is worked in one piece from cuff to cuff in variegated yarn.

SIZES

Sized for Small/Medium, Large/X-Large, XX-Large and shown in size Small/Medium.

KNITTED MEASUREMENTS

Bust 50 (54, 58)"/127 (137, 147)cm
Length 24 (24½, 25)"/61 (62, 63.5)cm
Upper arm 18 (19, 20)"/45.5 (48, 51)cm

MATERIALS

• 4 (5, 5) .88oz/25g balls (each approx 218yd/200m) of Debbie Bliss/KFI *Angel Prints* (mohair/silk) in #08 chagall (purples and pinks) **①**

• One pair each sizes 5 and 8 (3.75 and 5mm) needles OR SIZE TO OBTAIN GAUGE

• Stitch markers, stitch holders

GAUGE

18 sts and 24 rows = 4"/10cm over St st using larger needles.
TAKE TIME TO CHECK GAUGE.

LEFT SLEEVE

With smaller needles, cast on 50 (50, 55) sts. Work in k1, p1 rib for 3½"/9cm. Change to larger needles and work in St st as foll:

Row 1 (inc RS) Knit, inc 0 (4, 5) sts evenly across row—50 (54, 60) sts.

Row 2 (WS) P25 (27, 30), place marker (pm) and slip marker every row, p to end.

Row 3 (inc RS) K3, M1, k to 2 sts before marker, M1, k4, M1, k to last 3 sts, M1, k3.

Rows 4-6 Work even.

Row 7 (inc RS) K3, M1, k to last 3 sts, M1, k3.

Rows 8-10 Work even.

Rep rows 3–10 five times more, then rep rows 3–6 once—90 (94, 100) sts.

BODY

Side shaping

Cast on 6 sts at beg of next 4 rows.

Next (inc) row (RS) Cast on 6 sts, k to 2 sts before marker, M1, k4, M1, k to end. Cast on 6 sts at beg of next 7 rows—164 (168, 174) sts.

Next (inc) row (RS) Cast on 3 sts, k to 2 sts before marker, M1, k4, M1, k to end. Cast on 3 sts at beg of next 7 rows—190 (194, 200) sts. Rep last 8 rows once more—216 (220, 226) sts. Work 20 (26, 32) rows even, end with a WS row. Piece measures approx 20½ (21½, 22½)"/52 (54.5, 57)cm from cuff edge.

Divide for neck

Next row (RS) K108 (110, 113), turn. Place rem sts on stitch holder for front.

Next row (WS) K3, p to end.

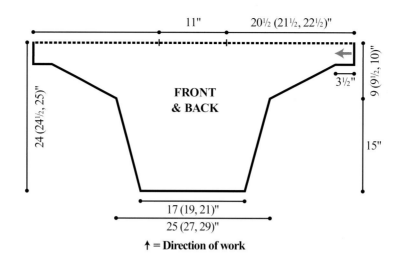

11"　　　20½ (21½, 22½)"

FRONT
& BACK

24 (24½, 25)"

9 (9½, 10)"

3½"

15"

17 (19, 21)"

25 (27, 29)"

↑ = Direction of work

Next row (RS) Knit. Rep last 2 rows until neck opening measures 11"/28cm, ending with a RS row. Place sts on stitch holder for back.

With RS facing, rejoin yarn to front sts and work as foll:

Next row (RS) Knit.

Next row (WS) P to last 3 sts, k3. Rep last 2 rows until neck opening measures same as back, end with a RS row.

Joining row (WS) P105 (107, 110), k3, pm, work back sts from st holder as foll: k3, p to end—216 (220, 226) sts. Work 20 (26, 32) rows even in St st, ending with a WS row. Piece measures approx 3¼ (4¼, 5¼)"/8 (11, 13.5)cm from neck opening.

Side shaping

Bind off 3 sts at beg of next 8 rows.

Next (dec) row (RS) Bind off 3 sts, k to 4 sts before marker, k2tog, k4, SKP, k to end. Bind off 3 sts at beg of next 7 rows.

Next (dec) row (RS) Bind off 6 sts, k to 4 sts before marker, k2tog, k4, SKP, k to end.

Bind off 6 sts at beg of next 7 rows.

Next (dec) row (RS) Bind off 6 sts, k to 4 sts before

marker, k2tog, k4, SKP, k to end. Bind off 6 sts at beg of next 3 rows—90 (94, 100) sts.

RIGHT SLEEVE

Work 4 rows even.

Dec row 1 (RS) K2, SKP, k to 4 sts before marker, k2tog, k4, SKP, k to last 4 sts, k2tog, k2.

Rows 2–4 Work even.

Dec row 5 (RS) K2, SKP, k to last 4 sts, k2tog, k2.

Rows 6–8 Work even.

Rep rows 1–8 five times more, then work dec row 1 once more—50 (54, 60) sts.

Next (dec) row (WS) Purl, dec 0 (4, 5) sts evenly across row—50 (50, 55) sts. Change to smaller needles and work in k1, p1 rib for 3½"/9cm. Bind off in rib.

FINISHING

With smaller needles and RS facing, pick up and k 75 (84, 93) sts along lower edge of front.

Knit 4 rows, bind off. Rep for lower edge of back.

Sew side and sleeve seams.

See schematic. ■

Turtleneck Tunic

Josh Bennett's oversized tunic is knit in two slope-shoulder pieces featuring intarsia bands at the hip.

SIZES

Sized for Small, Medium, Large, 1X, 2X and shown in size Medium.

KNITTED MEASUREMENTS

Bust 47 (49, 51, 53, 55)"/119.5 (124.5, 129.5, 134.5, 139.5)cm
Length 30 (31, 32, 33, 34)"/76 (78.5, 81, 83.5, 86.5)cm

MATERIALS

• 7 (7, 8, 8, 9) 4oz/113g skeins (each approx 190yd/173m) of Brown Sheep Company *Lamb's Pride Worsted* in M77 blue magic (A) 🔲

• 1 skein in M06 deep charcoal (B)

• Small amount in M162 mulberry (C)

• One pair each sizes 8 and 10½ (5 and 6.5mm) needles OR SIZE TO OBTAIN GAUGE

• Sizes 8 and 10½ (5 and 6.5mm) circular needle, each 16"/40cm long

• Stitch markers

GAUGE

16 sts and 22 rows = 4"/10cm over St st using larger needles.
TAKE TIME TO CHECK GAUGE.

STITCH GLOSSARY

Inc 2 K1, p1, k1 into same st to inc 2 sts in rib.

K1, P1 RIB

(over an even number of sts)
Row 1 *K1, p1; rep from * to end.
Row 2 K the knit sts and p the purl sts.
Rep row 2 for k1, p1 rib.

BACK

With smaller needles and A, cast on 94 (98, 102, 106, 110) sts. Work in k1, p1 rib until piece measures 1"/2.5cm from beg, end with a WS row. Change to larger needles.

Work 16 rows in St st (k on RS, p on WS).

Beg stripes

Cont in St st work 2 rows B, 6 rows A, 14 rows B, 6 rows A, 2 rows C.

Cont in A only until piece measures 24 (25, 26, 27, 28)"/61 (63.5, 66, 68.5, 71)cm from beg, end with a WS row.

Shoulder shaping

Next (dec) row (RS) K2tog, k to last 2 sts, ssk—92 (96, 100, 104, 108) sts. Rep dec row every other row 13 times more—66 (70, 74, 78, 82) sts. Work 1 row even.

Bind off 6 (6, 8, 8, 8) sts at beg of next 2 rows, 6 (7, 7, 7, 8) sts at beg of next 4 rows. Bind off rem 30 (30, 30, 34, 34) sts.

FRONT

Work same as for back until the 14 shoulder dec rows are complete—66 (70, 74, 78, 82) sts.

Shape neck

Next row (RS) K24 (26, 28, 28, 30), join 2nd ball of yarn and bind off center 18 (18, 18, 22, 22) sts, k to end.

Working both sides at once, bind off 2 sts from each neck edge 3 times, AT SAME TIME, cont to shape shoulders same as for back.

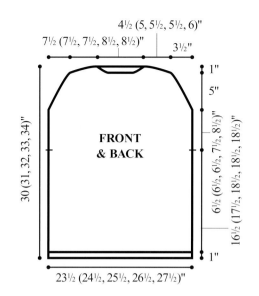

FRONT & BACK

4½ (5, 5½, 5½, 6)"
7½ (7½, 7½, 8½, 8½)"
3½"
1"
5"
6½ (6½, 6½, 7½, 8½)"
30 (31, 32, 33, 34)"
16½ (17½, 18½, 18½, 18½)"
1"
23½ (24½, 25½, 26½, 27½)"

FINISHING

Sew shoulder seams. Place a marker on each side edge of front and back 6½ (6½, 6½, 7½, 8½)"/16.5 (16.5, 16.5, 19, 21.5)cm down from shoulders. With smaller needles and A, pick up and k 68 (68, 68, 76, 92) sts evenly between markers. Work in k1, p1 rib for 1"/2.5cm. Bind off in pat. Sew side seams, including armhole bands.

Turtleneck

With smaller circular needle and A, pick up and k 72 (72, 72, 78, 78) sts evenly around neck edge. Join and pm for beg of rnd. Work 3 rnds in k1, p1 rib.

Next (inc) rnd *Inc 2 into next st, [p1, k1] twice, p1; rep from * around—96 (96, 96, 104, 104) sts. Cont in k1, p1 rib until turtleneck measures 4"/10cm from beg. Change to larger circular needle. Work even in pat until turtleneck measures 9½"/24cm from beg. Bind off loosely in pat. ◼

Oversized Poncho

"P" is for poncho! Marcia Cleary's long, lush poncho carries an allover knit/purl pattern in a basketweave stitch trimmed with broken ribbing.

SIZES

Sized for Small/Medium, Large/X-Large, 2X/3X and shown in Size 2X/3X.

KNITTED MEASUREMENTS

Width across front 44 (48, 52)"/111.5 (122, 132)cm

Length 28 (28, 30)"/71 (71, 76)cm

MATERIALS

• 15 (16, 17) 3½oz/100g hanks (each approx 109yd/100m) of Plymouth Yarn Co. *DeAire* (wool) in #100 off white ⑥

• Size 13 (9mm) circular needles, one each 16"/40cm and 24"/60cm long, OR SIZE TO OBTAIN GAUGE

• Size 15 (10mm) circular needle, 16"/40cm long

• Stitch markers

GAUGE

12 sts and 18 rows = 4"/10cm over basketweave pat using size 13 (9mm) needle.

TAKE TIME TO CHECK GAUGE.

BROKEN RIB STITCH (in rows)

(over an even number of sts)

Row 1 (WS) *K1, p1; rep from * to end.

Row 2 Knit.

Rep rows 1 and 2 for broken rib st in rows.

BROKEN RIB STITCH (in rnds)

(over an even number of sts)

Rnd 1 (RS) *K1, p1; rep from * to end.

Rnd 2 (RS) Purl.

Rep rnds 1 and 2 for broken rib st in rnds.

BASKETWEAVE PATTERN

(multiple of 12 sts)

Rows 1, 3, 5, and 7 (WS) *K2, p2, k2, k6; rep from * to end.

Rows 2, 4, 6, and 8 *K6, p2, k2, p2; rep from * to end.

Rows 9, 11, 13, and 15 *K6, k2, p2, k2; rep from * to end.

Rows 10, 12, 14, and 16 *P2, k2, p2, k6; rep from * to end.

Rep rows 1–16 for basketweave pat.

NOTE

Circular needles are used to accommodate the large number of sts. Work back and forth in rows, except for the collar.

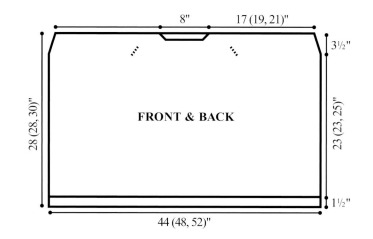

8"   17 (19, 21)"

3½"

28 (28, 30)"

FRONT & BACK

23 (23, 25)"

1½"

44 (48, 52)"

BACK

With size 13 (9mm) 24"/60cm circular needle, cast on 132 (144, 156) sts. Work broken rib st in rows for 1½"/4cm.

Beg basketweave pat

Next row (WS) Cont first 6 sts in broken rib st, work basketweave pat to last 6 sts, cont broken rib st to end. Cont in pats as established until 16 rows of pat have been worked 6 (6, 7) times, then rep rows 1–7 once (once, 0) more—piece measures approx 24½ (24½, 26½)"/62 (62, 67)cm from beg.

Inner darts

Next row (RS) Work 39 (45, 51) sts, place marker (pm), k2tog, work to last 41 (47, 53) sts, ssk, pm, work to end.

Next row (WS) Work to marker, slip marker (sm), bring yarn to front and sl next st, bring yarn to back and cont in pat to 1 st before next marker, bring yarn to front and slip next st, sm, work to end. Rep last 2 rows twice more—126 (138, 150) sts.

Next row (RS) Work to marker, sm, k1, work to 1 st before next marker, k1, sm, work to end.

Next row (WS) Work as before, slipping sts at markers. Rep last 2 rows until 16 pat rows have been worked from beg of inner darts—piece measures approx 28 (28, 30)"/71 (71, 76)cm from beg. Bind off all sts.

FRONT

Work as for back until 5 rows fewer than back.

Neck shaping

Next row (RS) Work 53 (59, 65) sts, join 2nd ball of yarn and bind off center 20 sts, work to end. Working both sides at once, [dec 1 st at each neck edge on next WS row, work 1 row even] twice. Bind off rem 51 (57, 63) sts each side knitwise on WS for shoulder/sleeves.

FINISHING

Do *not* block. With RS tog, sew bound-off edge of front and back tog for shoulder/sleeve seams, leaving neck open. Turn poncho inside out (so seam is on WS).

Collar

With RS facing and size 13 (9mm) 16"/40cm circular needle, pick up and k 26 sts along back neck and 30 sts along front neck—56 sts. Join and place marker for beg of rnd. Work broken rib st in rnds for 4"/10cm. Change to size 15 (10mm) 16"/40cm needle and work 2"/5cm more, end with a pat rnd 1. Bind off loosely purlwise. ◼

Shawl Collar Cardi

Jacqueline van Dillen's boldly cabled cardigan boasts ridge-patterned front bands that form a shawl collar.

SIZES

Sized for Small, Medium, Large, X-Large, XX-Large and shown in size Small.

KNITTED MEASUREMENTS

Bust (closed) 35 (41½, 44½, 51½, 54)"/89 (105.5, 113, 131, 137)cm

Length 29½ (30, 30½, 31, 31½)"/74.5 (76, 77, 78, 79)cm

Upper arm 14 (14, 14, 16¾, 16¾)"/35.5 (35.5, 35.5, 42.5, 42.5)cm

MATERIALS

• 13 (14, 16, 18, 19) 3½oz/100g hanks (each approx 127yd/116m) of Classic Elite Yarns *Montera* (llama/wool) in #3877 smoke (5)

• One pair size 11 (8mm) needles, OR SIZE TO OBTAIN GAUGE

• Stitch markers and holders

• Cable needle (cn)

GAUGE

20 sts and 18 rows = 4"/10cm over chart pat using size 11 (8mm) needles.
TAKE TIME TO CHECK GAUGE.

STITCH GLOSSARY

8-st RC Sl 4 sts to cn and hold to back, k4, k4 from cn.

8-st LC Sl 4 sts to cn and hold to front, k4, k4 from cn.

RIDGE PATTERN

*K 2 rows, p 2 rows; rep from * (4 rows) for ridge pat.

BACK

Cast on 114 (128, 142, 156, 170) sts. Work in k2, p2 for 4 rows.

Beg chart pat

Row 1 (RS) Beg with st 1, work 28-st rep 4 (4, 5, 5, 6) times, then work first 14 sts of rep 0 (once, 0, once, 0) more, work last 2 sts of chart. Cont in pat as established until piece measures 4"/10cm from beg.

Side shaping

Dec 1 st each side on next row (working dec sts into pat), then every 4th row 1 (6, 6, 12, 12) times more, every 6th row 9 (6, 6, 2, 2) times—92 (102, 116, 126, 140) sts. Work even until piece measures 20¾"/52.5cm from beg.

Raglan armhole shaping

Bind off 5 (6, 6, 7, 8) sts at beg of next 2 rows.

* Yarn used in original pattern is no longer available and is listed on page 190.

Dec 2 sts each side (by working k3tog) every other row 0 (2, 8, 10, 15) times—82 (82, 72, 72, 64) sts. Dec 1 st each side every other row 19 (18, 13, 12, 8) times. Bind off rem 44 (46, 46, 48, 48) sts on next RS row.

LEFT FRONT

Cast on 58 (72, 72, 86, 86) sts.

Next row (RS) Beg with k2 (p2, p2, k2, k2), work in k2, p2 rib over 44 (58, 58, 72, 72) sts, ending with p2, pm, work ridge pat over last 14 sts. Cont in pats as established for 3 rows more.

Beg chart pat

Row 1 (RS) Beg with st 1 (15, 1, 15, 1), work chart to last 16 sts, work last 2 sts of chart, sl marker, cont ridge pat over last 14 sts. Cont in pats as established until piece measures 4"/10cm from beg.

Side, collar and armhole shaping

Note Read before beg to knit.

Dec 1 st at beg of next RS row (side edge), then every 4th row 1 (6, 6, 12, 12) times more, every 6th row 9 (6, 6, 2, 2) times, AT SAME TIME, when piece measures 12"/30cm from beg, inc for collar as foll:

Next row (RS) Work to marker, sl marker, M1 (or M1 p-st, depending on ridge pat row), work ridge pat to end. Rep this inc every 4th row 15 times more, AT SAME TIME, when same length as back to armhole, shape armhole at side edge (beg of RS rows) as for back. After all shaping has been completed there are 39 (47, 40, 48, 41) sts. Bind off 9 (17, 10, 18, 11) sts at beg of next RS row for shoulder. Place rem 30 sts on holder.

RIGHT FRONT

Cast on 58 (72, 72, 86, 86) sts.

Next row (RS) Work ridge pat over first 14 sts, pm, beg with p2, work in k2, p2 rib over last 44 (58, 58, 72, 72) sts, end with k2 (p2, p2, k2, k2). Cont in pats as established for 3 rows more.

Beg chart pat

Row 1 (RS) Cont ridge pat over first 14 sts, sl marker, beg with st 15 (1, 1, 15, 15) work chart to last 2 sts, work last 2 sts of chart.

Complete to correspond to left front, reversing all shaping.

SLEEVES

Cast on 72 (72, 72, 86, 86) sts. Work in k2, p2 rib for 4"/10cm.

Beg cable pat

Next row (RS) Work 28-st rep 2 (2, 2, 3, 3) times, work first 14 sts once (once, once, 0, 0) more, work last 2 sts of chart. Cont in pat as established until piece measures 16 (16½, 16½, 17, 17)"/40.5 (42, 42, 43, 43)cm from beg.

Raglan cap shaping

Bind off 5 (6, 6, 7, 8) sts at beg of next 2 rows.
Dec 2 sts each side (by k3tog) every other row 3 (1, 0, 5, 3) times—50 (56, 60, 52, 58) sts.
Dec 1 st each side every other row 16 (19, 21, 17, 20) times. Bind off rem 18 sts.

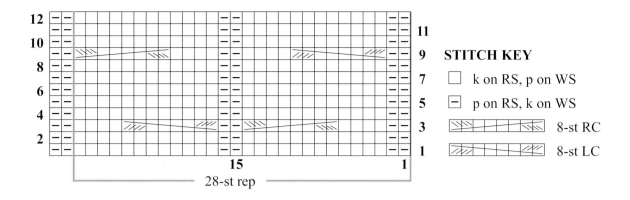

STITCH KEY

☐ k on RS, p on WS

⊟ p on RS, k on WS

8-st RC

8-st LC

12 | 11
10 | 9
8 | 7
6 | 5
4 | 3
2 | 1

15 | **1**

28-st rep

FINISHING

Block pieces lightly to measurements.

Sew shoulder seams.

Back collar

Slip sts from left front holder to needle and cont in ridge pat until piece fits along one half of back neck. Place sts on holder. Work sts on right front holder in same way. Sew open sts of two collar pieces tog. Sew sides of collar along back neck edge.

Sew raglan sleeve caps into raglan armholes. Sew side and sleeve seams. ■

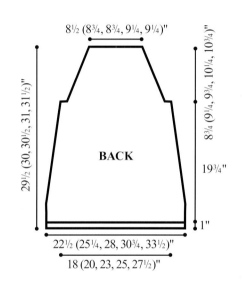

8½ (8¾, 8¾, 9¼, 9¼)"

8¾ (9¼, 9¾, 10¼, 10¾)"

29½ (30, 30½, 31, 31½)"

BACK

8¾ (9¼, 9¾, 10¼, 10¾)"

19¾"

1"

22½ (25¼, 28, 30¾, 33½)"

18 (20, 23, 25, 27½)"

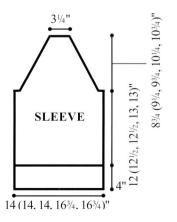

3¼"

8¾ (9¼, 9¾, 10¼, 10¾)"

12 (12½, 12½, 13, 13)"

SLEEVE

4"

14 (14, 14, 16¾, 16¾)"

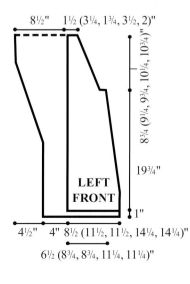

8½"   1½ (3¼, 1¾, 3½, 2)"

8¾ (9¼, 9¾, 10¼, 10¾)"

19¾"

LEFT FRONT

1"

4½"   4"   8½ (11½, 11½, 14¼, 14¼)"

6½ (8¾, 8¾, 11¼, 11¼)"

Cable Front Cardi

Sarah Hatton's cropped capelike cardigan boasts just the right amount of fashion flourish. It features batwing sleeves, a stand-up collar and snap closures up the cabled front.

SIZES

Sized for Small/Medium, Large/X-Large, 1X/2X and shown in size Small/Medium.

KNITTED MEASUREMENTS

Waist (closed) 36 (40, 44)"/91.5 (101.5, 111.5)cm*
Length 18 (20, 21½)"/45.5 (51, 54.5)cm
Upper arm (cuff edge) 22 (24½, 26½)"/56 (62, 67)cm
The "bust" measurement that traditionally determines fit actually reflects the measurement that is taken around the "waist edge" (see photo).

MATERIALS

• 10 (12, 14) 1¾oz/50g balls (each approx 54yd/49m) of Schachenmayr Select/Westminster Fibers *Diverso* (wool/mohair/nylon) in #7546 burgundy ⑥

• One pair each sizes 11 and 15 (8 and 10mm) needles OR SIZE TO OBTAIN GAUGE

• Cable needle (cn)

• Stitch holders

• Five ¾"/20mm snap closures

GAUGE

11 sts and 14 rows = 4"/10cm over St st using size 15 (10mm) needles.
TAKE TIME TO CHECK GAUGE.

STITCH GLOSSARY

3-st RC Sl 1 st to cn and hold to *back*, k2, k1 from cn.
3-st LC Sl 2 sts to cn and hold to *front*, k1, k2 from cn.
4-st RC Sl 2 sts to cn and hold to *back*, k2, k2 from cn.
4-st LC Sl 2 sts to cn and hold to *front*, k2, k2 from cn.

BACK

With smaller needles, cast on 49 (55, 61) sts.
For sizes S/M and 1X/2X—Row 1 (RS) K2, *p3, k3; rep from *, end k2 instead of k3.
For size L/XL—Row 1 (RS) P2, *k3, p3; rep from *, end p2 instead of p3.
For all sizes
Cont in k3, p3 rib as established for 9 rows more. Change to larger needles.

Raglan armhole shaping

Dec row 1 (RS) K1, ssk, k to last 3 sts, k2tog, k1.
Row 2 Purl.
Row 3 Knit.
Row 4 Purl.
Rep rows 1–4 for 11 (12, 12) times more.
Next row (RS) Rep dec row 1.
Next row Purl.
Rep last 2 rows 2 (4, 6) times more. Bind off rem 19 (19, 21) sts.

LEFT FRONT

With smaller needles, cast on 28 (31, 34) sts.

Row 1 (RS) K2 (p2, k2), k0 (3, 0), *p3, k3; rep from * to last 8 sts, end p4, k1, p1, k2.

Row 2 (WS) [K1, p1] twice, k4, *p3, k3; rep from *, end p0 (3, 0), p2 (k2, p2).

Cont in established rib for 7 rows more.

Next row (WS) [K1, p1] twice, k4, p1, inc 1 st in next st, p1, k3, work in rib to last st, inc 1 st in last st—30 (33, 36) sts. Change to larger needles.

Beg chart 1

Dec row 1 (RS) K1, ssk, k11 (14, 17), work 12 sts foll row 1 of chart 1, k1, p1, k2.

Row 2 (WS) [K1, p1] twice, work 12 sts in chart 1, purl to end.

Row 3 K to last 16 sts, work chart 1, k1, p1, k2.

Row 4 Rep row 2.

Cont in this manner to work rows 1–8 of chart 1 to the completion of the front, AT SAME TIME, rep these dec rows 1–4 for 12 (13, 12) times more—17 (19, 23) sts.

Next row Work even.

Rep last 2 rows 0 (2, 6) times more—16 sts.

There are same number of rows as back armhole. Sl sts to a holder.

RIGHT FRONT

With smaller needles, cast on 28 (31, 34) sts.

Row 1 (RS) K2, p1, k1, p4, *k3, p3; rep from *, end k0 (3, 0), k2 (p2, k2).

Cont in established rib for 8 rows more.

Next row (WS) Inc 1 st in first st, work rib to last 11 sts, p1, inc 1 st in next st, p1, k4, [p1, k1] twice—30 (33, 36) sts. Change to larger needles.

Beg chart 2

Dec row 1 (RS) K2, p1, k1, work 12 sts foll row 1 of chart 2, k to last 3 sts, k2tog, k1.

Row 2 (WS) Purl to last 16 sts, work 12 sts of chart 2, [p1, k1] twice.

Row 3 Work even.

Row 4 Rep row 2.

Cont in this manner to work rows 1–8 of chart 2 to the completion of the front, AT SAME TIME, rep these dec rows 1–4 for 12 (13, 12) times more—17 (19, 23) sts.

Next row (RS) Rep dec row 1.

Next row Work even.

Rep last 2 rows 0 (2, 6) times more—16 sts. There are same numbers of rows as back armhole. Sl sts to a holder.

CHART 1

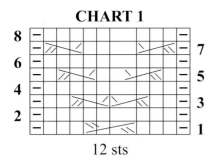

12 sts

CHART 2

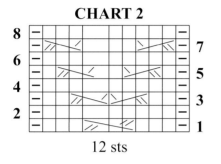

12 sts

Stitch Key

☐	k on RS, p on WS	⊠	3-st LT
⊟	p on RS, k on WS	⊠	4-st RC
⊠	3-st RT	⊠	4-st LC

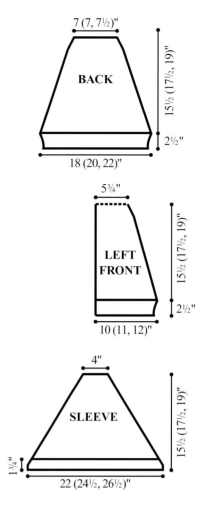

SLEEVES

With smaller needles, cast on 61 (67, 73) sts. Beg and end with k2, work in k3, p3 rib for 2 rows.

Raglan cap shaping

Dec row 1 (RS) K1, ssk, work to last 3 sts, k2tog, k1. Work 3 rows even. Change to larger needles and cont in St st and raglan shaping as foll:

For size L/XL only Rep dec row 1. Work 3 rows even.

For all sizes Rep dec row 1. Work 1 row even. Rep last 2 rows 23 (25, 29) times more. Bind off rem 11 sts.

FINISHING

Sew raglan sleeve caps into raglan armholes.

Collar

With smaller needles, beg at right front band, work k1, [k1, p1] 7 times, k1 from holder, pick up and k 11 sts from top of sleeve, 19 (19, 21) sts from back neck, 11 sts from top of left sleeve, then work k1, [p1, k1] 7 times, k1 from left front neck—73 (73, 75) sts. Cont in k1, p1 rib as established for 2¾"/7cm. Bind off in rib. Sew the side seams in the rib section of back and front. Mark places for the 5 snaps evenly spaced along the fronts. Sew snaps in place. ■

Belted Dolman Sweater

Openings on either side of twin bands of cabling allow a belt to cinch though Ruth Garcia-Alcantud's dolman pullover, knit in pieces from side to side.

SIZES

Sized for Small, Medium, Large, X-Large, XX-Large and shown in size Small.

KNITTED MEASUREMENTS

Bust 37 (40, 44, 48, 52)"/94 (101.5, 111.5, 122, 132)cm

Length 23 (23, 24, 24, 25)"/58.5 (58.5, 61, 61, 63.5)cm

Upper arm 16 (16, 18, 18, 19½)"/40.5 (40.5, 45.5, 45.5, 49.5)cm

Cable panel 2"/5cm wide x 46 (46, 48, 48, 49¾)"/117 (117, 122, 122, 126)cm long

MATERIALS

• 6 (7, 8, 8, 9) 3½oz/100g hanks (each approx 218yd/199m) of Plymouth Yarn Co. *Worsted Merino Superwash* (wool) in #12 olive (4)

• One pair each sizes 9 and 10 (5.5 and 6mm) needles OR SIZE TO OBTAIN GAUGE

• Two size 9 (5.5mm) double-pointed needles (dpns)

• Cable needle (cn)

• Stitch markers

GAUGE

18 sts and 26 rows = 4"/10cm over St st using size 9 (5.5mm) needles.

TAKE TIME TO CHECK GAUGE.

STITCH GLOSSARY

4-st RC Sl 2 sts to cn and hold to *back*, k2, k2 from cn.

4-ST LC Sl 2 sts to cn and hold to *front*, k2, k2 from cn.

CABLE PATTERN

(over 16 sts)

Row 1 (RS) K3, [4-st LC] 3 times, k1.

Rows 2 and 4 (WS) Purl.

Row 3 (RS) K1, [4-st RC] 3 times, k3.

Rep rows 1–4 for cable pat.

CABLE PANELS (make 2)

With larger needles, cast on 16 sts. K one row, p one row, then work in cable pat until piece measures 45¾ (45¾, 47¾, 47¾, 49½)"/116 (116, 121, 121, 125.5)cm from beg, end with a row 4. K one row, p one row. Bind off.

Block panels to measurements. Place markers (pm) 5"/12.5cm and 7"/18cm from each end for belt openings. Pm 23 (23, 24, 24, 24¾)"/58.5 (58.5, 61, 61, 63)cm from end for shoulder.

SIDE AND SLEEVE

With smaller needles and RS facing, pick up and k 22 sts along edge of cable panel to first belt loop marker, cast on 9 sts, pick up and k 73 (73, 77, 77, 81) sts from second belt loop marker to shoulder, 73 (73, 77, 77, 81) sts from shoulder to next belt opening marker, cast on 9 sts, pick up and k 22 sts from last belt opening marker to lower edge—208 (208, 216, 216, 224) sts.

Next row (WS) Knit.

Next row (RS) Purl.

Cont in rev St st (k on WS, p on RS) until piece measures 3 (3¾, 4¾, 5¾, 6¾)"/7.5 (9.5, 12, 14.5, 17)cm from panel edge, end with a RS row.

Shape sleeve

Bind off 68 sts at beg of next 2 rows—72 (72, 80, 80, 88) sts. Pm at end of 2nd row for sleeve, do not slip this marker.

Dec 1 st at each end of every other row 8 (8, 15, 15, 20) times, then every 4th row 5 (5, 2, 2, 1) times—46 sts. Work even until piece measures 14 (14, 14½, 14½, 15)"/35.5 (35.5, 37, 37, 38)cm from sleeve marker, end with a WS row.

Next row (RS) P2, *k2, p2; rep from * to end.

Work in p2, k2 rib as established until sleeve measures 18 (18, 18½, 18½, 19)"/45.5 (45.5, 47, 47, 48)cm from marker. Bind off.

Rep side and sleeve for 2nd cable panel.

FRONT

Note Sides and sleeves are the same, select one to be the left side and sleeve and work as foll:

With smaller needles and RS facing, beg at shoulder, pick up and k 73 (73, 77, 77, 81) sts

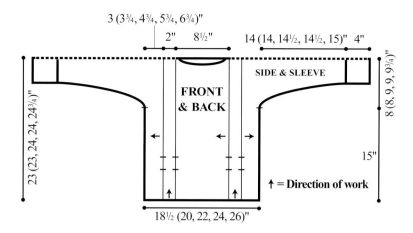

3 (3¾, 4¾, 5¾, 6¾)"
2"   8½"
14 (14, 14½, 14½, 15)"   4"

SIDE & SLEEVE

FRONT & BACK

8 (8, 9, 9¾)"

23 (23, 24, 24, 24¾)"

15"

↑ = Direction of work

18½ (20, 22, 24, 26)"

along edge of cable panel from shoulder to first belt opening marker, cast on 9 sts, pick up and k 22 sts from lower belt opening marker to lower edge—104 (104, 108, 108, 112) sts.

Work 4 rows in rev St st.

Neck shaping

Dec 1 st at neck edge on next row, then every 4th row 4 times more—99 (99, 103, 103, 107) sts. Work even until piece measures 4¾"/12cm from cable panel.

Inc 1 st at neck edge on next row, then every 4th row 4 times more—104 (104, 108, 108, 112) sts. Work even until piece measures 8½"/21.5cm. Bind off.

BACK

With smaller needles and RS facing, beg at lower edge of left cable panel, pick up and k 22 sts along edge of cable panel from lower edge to first belt opening marker, cast on 9 sts, pick up and k 73 (73, 77, 77, 81) sts from second belt opening marker to shoulder—104 (104, 108, 108, 112) sts. Work in rev St st until piece measures 8½"/21.5cm. Bind off.

FINISHING

Block all pieces to measurements. Sew edge of right cable panel to front and back, leaving opening between markers for belt. Sew side and sleeve seams.

Lower edging

With dpn, cast on 3 sts and, beg at side seam, work attached I-cord along lower edge as foll: *K2, pick up and k 1 st along edge, knit the 3rd st tog with picked-up st. Do not turn, slide sts to opposite end of needle to work next row from RS. Pull yarn tightly from end of row. Rep from * around entire lower edge. Cut yarn, pull through 3 sts and fasten off.

Neck edging

With dpn, cast on 4 sts. Beg at shoulder, work attached I-cord along neck edge as foll: *K3, pick up and k 1 st along edge, knit the 4th st tog with picked-up st. Do not turn, slide sts to opposite end of needle to work next row from RS. Pull yarn tightly from end of row. Rep from * around neck edge. Cut yarn, pull through 4 sts and fasten off. ■

Cabled Dolman

A little Alpine flair dresses up the weekend. Josh Bennett's creamy cabled sweater is worked in a big rectangle from cuff to cuff and is cleverly divided so that the cables continue unbroken along the neckline edge.

SIZES

Sized for Small, Medium, Large and shown in size Small.

KNITTED MEASUREMENTS

Waist circumference 30 (38, 44)"/76 (96.5, 111.5)cm

Length 18¾"/47.5cm

Upper arm 27½"/70cm

MATERIALS

• 16 (17, 17) 1¾oz/50g hanks (each approx 150yd/135m) of Manos del Uruguay/Fairmount Fibers *Silk Blend* (wool/silk) in #3014 natural (3)

• One pair size 10 (6mm) needles OR SIZE TO OBTAIN GAUGES

• Size 9 (5.5mm) circular needle, 29"/74cm long

• Stitch holders, stitch markers, and cable needle (cn)

GAUGES

16 sts and 24 rows = 4"/10cm over St st using larger needles.

One 20-st cable panel = 3½"/9cm width.

TAKE TIME TO CHECK GAUGES.

STITCH GLOSSARY

6-st RC (LC) Sl 3 sts to cn and hold to back (front), k3, k3 from cn.

8-st RC (LC) Sl 4 sts to cn and hold to back (front), k4, k4 from cn.

NOTE

The length and width of the main piece is the same for all 3 sizes. Only the waist circumference (and the opening at the lower edge) is different. Garment is worked with yarn held double throughout.

MAIN PIECE

Beg at the right sleeve opening edge, with size 10 (6mm) needles, cast on 140 sts.

Set up patterns

Row 1 (RS) P4, *work 20 sts of row 1 of chart 1, p8; rep from * 3 times more, work 20 sts of row 1 of chart 1, p4.

Row 2 (WS) K4, *work 20 sts of row 2 of cable chart 1, k8; rep from * 3 times more, work 20 sts of row 2 of chart 1, k4.

Cont to foll chart pat and work rem sts in rev St st as established until piece measures 16"/40.5cm from beg, end with pat row 12 of chart 1.

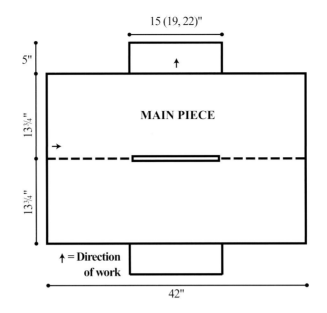

15 (19, 22)"

5"

↑

MAIN PIECE

13¾"

13¾"

↑ = **Direction of work**

42"

Divide for neck opening

Row 1 (RS) P4, [work 20 sts of row 1 of cable chart 1, p8] twice, k8, k2tog, turn, leaving the rem 70 sts on holder for back.

FRONT

Row 2 (WS) P9, work rem sts as established.

Row 3 (RS) Work as established to the last 9 sts, work row 3 of chart 2 over the last 9 sts.

Cont as established on these 69 sts for approx 10"/25.5cm, end with a chart 1 row 12. Leave the front sts on holder.

BACK

Return to the 70 sts on holder for the back.

Row 1 (RS) Ssk, k8, work to end. Complete the back neck as for the front neck, end with the same row as the front.

Join front and back

Next row (RS) Work the 69 sts of front in established pats foll row 1 of chart 1, inc 1 st at end, then inc 1

st in next st of beg of back and cont to end—140 sts. Work in chart 1 and rev St st pats as before on these sts until there are same number of rows as the first half. Bind off loosely.

FINISHING

Block lightly. Fold piece in half lengthwise and place markers to mark the center of the body front and back at the lower edge. Place markers at 7½ (9½, 11)"/19 (24, 28)cm each side of the center markers. Seam the sleeve up to these markers, leaving an opening of 15 (19, 22)"/38 (48, 56)cm on each piece.

Waistband

With circular needle, pick up and k 66 (83, 97) sts from front lower edge and 66 (83, 97) sts from back lower edge—132 (166, 194) sts. Join and pm to mark beg of rnd. Work in rnds of k1, p1 rib for 5"/12.5 cm. Bind off in rib. ■

CHART 1

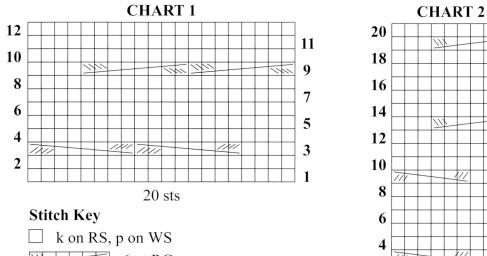

12
10
8
6
4
2

11
9
7
5
3
1

20 sts

CHART 2

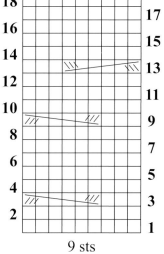

20
18
16
14
12
10
8
6
4
2

19
17
15
13
11
9
7
5
3
1

9 sts

Stitch Key

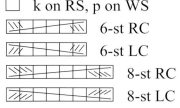

☐ k on RS, p on WS

⬭ 6-st RC

⬭ 6-st LC

⬭ 8-st RC

⬭ 8-st LC

Slouchy Pullover

Jumbo half-twist cables travel up the right side and through the collar of Tom Scott's slouchy slate tunic. The body, collar and picked-up short sleeves are knit in the round.

SIZES

Sized for X-Small, Small, Medium, Large and shown in size X-Small.

KNITTED MEASUREMENTS

Bust 33 (36, 39, 43)"/84 (91.5, 99, 109.5)cm
Length from top of collar 35 (35½, 36, 36½)"/89 (90, 91.5, 92.5)cm
Upper arm 14 (15, 16, 17)"/35.5 (38, 40.5, 43)cm

MATERIALS

• 12 (14, 15, 17) 3½oz/100g balls (each approx 110yd/100m) of Plymouth Yarn Co. *Baby Alpaca Grande* (superfine baby alpaca) in #401 gray ⑤

• One size 13 (9mm) circular needle, 29 (32, 32, 40)"/74 (80, 80, 100)cm long, OR SIZE TO OBTAIN GAUGES

• One set (4) size 13 (9mm) double-pointed needles (dpns)

• Large cable needle (cn) or dpn

• Stitch markers

GAUGES

10 sts and 14 rnds = 4"/10cm over St st using size 13 (9mm) needle and 2 strands of yarn.
20 sts cable = 4½"/11.5cm over cable pat.
TAKE TIME TO CHECK GAUGES.

STITCH GLOSSARY

20-st Front Cross (FC) Sl 10 sts to cn and hold to *front*, k10, twist sts on cn 180 degrees to the right, k10 from cn.

CABLE PATTERN (over 20 sts)

Rnds 1–9 K20.
Rnd 10 Work 20-st FC.
Rnds 11–28 K20.
Rnd 29 Work 20-st FC.
Rnds 30–52 K20.
Rnd 53 Work 20-st FC.
Rnds 54–78 K20.
Rnd 79 Work 20-st FC.
Rnds 80–102 K20.
Rnd 103 Work 20-st FC.
Work in St st to end of piece.

BODY

With 2 strands of yarn held tog, cast on 100 (108, 116, 124) sts. Join, taking care not to twist sts on needle, and place marker for beg of rnd.
Rnd 1 P25 (27, 29, 31), k20 (for cable pat), p5 (7, 9, 11), pm for end of front, p25 (27, 29, 31), k20 (for cable pat), p5 (7, 9, 11). Cont in pats as established and working sts outside of cable pat in rev St st, until piece measures 16"/40.5cm from beg.

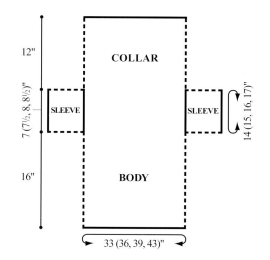

COLLAR

SLEEVE

SLEEVE

BODY

12"

7 (7½, 8, 8½)"

16"

14 (15, 16, 17)"

33 (36, 39, 43)"

Divide for armhole

Next row (RS) Work 50 (54, 58, 62) sts for front, place rem sts on a holder. Working back and forth in rows, cont in pats until armhole measures 7 (7½, 8, 8½)"/17.5 (19, 20.5, 21.5)cm. Place sts on a holder. Sl sts from back holder to needle and work as for front. Join front and back again and cont in rnds for 12"/30.5cm. Bind off all sts in pat.

SLEEVES

With RS facing, dpn and 2 strands of yarn, pick up and k 36 (38, 40, 42) sts evenly around each armhole opening. Join and work in rnds of St st for 6"/15.5cm. Bind off all sts. ■

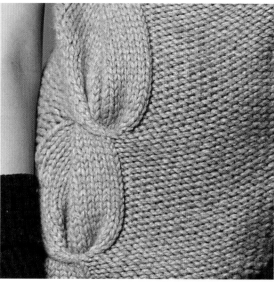

Cowl Neck Mohair Sweater

Cables take on an Impressionistic quality when softened by mohair. In this case, Ellen Ligouri uses a soft lilac for her tunic, balancing a generously cushy cowl neck with wide ribbed sleeves.

SIZES

Sized for Small, Medium/Large, X-Large, 1X and shown in size Medium/Large.

KNITTED MEASUREMENTS

Bust 40½ (45½, 50½, 55½)"/103 (115.5, 128, 141)cm
Length 25½ (26, 26½, 27)"/65 (66, 67, 68.5)cm
Upper arm 23 (24, 25, 26)"/58.5 (61, 63.5, 66)cm

MATERIALS

• 10 (11, 12, 14) 1¾oz/50g hanks (each approx 115yd/105m) of Kollàge Yarns *Whimsy* (mohair/nylon/wool) in #7002 cadet blue (4)

• Sizes 9 and 10 (5.5 and 6mm) circular needles, each 60"/150cm long, OR SIZE TO OBTAIN GAUGE

• Sizes 8, 9, 10, 10½, 11, and 13 (5, 5.5, 6, 6.5, 8, and 9mm) circular needles, each 16"/40cm long

• Cable needle (cn), stitch markers

GAUGE

16 sts and 20 rows = 4"/10cm over cable pat using size 10 (6mm) needle.
TAKE TIME TO CHECK GAUGE.

STITCH GLOSSARY

4-st RC Sl 2 sts to cn, hold to *back,* k2, k2 from cn.

BACK

Note Circular needle is used to accommodate large number of sts. Do not join.

With size 9 (5.5mm) needle, cast on 60 (68, 76, 84) sts. Work in k1, p1 rib for 4"/10cm, end with a RS row.

Inc row (WS) Purl, inc 21 (23, 25, 27) sts evenly spaced across—81 (91, 101, 111) sts.

Beg cable pat

Change to size 10 (6mm) needle.
Row 1 (RS) Beg with st 1, work 10-st rep of chart 8 (9, 10, 11) times, end with st 11. Cont in chart pat, rep rows 1–24 until piece measures 9"/23cm from beg. Working inc sts into pat, inc 1 st each side every RS row 10 times—101 (111, 121, 131) sts.

SLEEVES

Next row (WS) Cast on 39 sts, then p1, [k1, p1] 19 times across these sts, work chart pat to end.

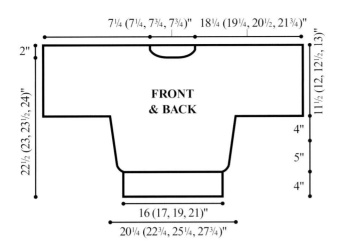

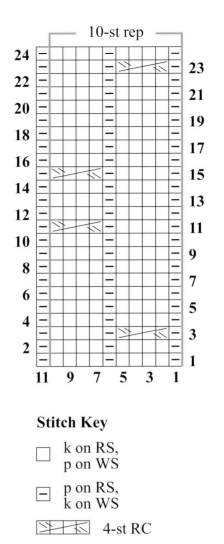

10-st rep

Row numbers on left: 24, 22, 20, 18, 16, 14, 12, 10, 8, 6, 4, 2
Row numbers on right: 23, 21, 19, 17, 15, 13, 11, 9, 7, 5, 3, 1
Column numbers on bottom: 11, 9, 7, 5, 3, 1

Stitch Key

☐ k on RS,
p on WS

⊟ p on RS,
k on WS

▨ 4-st RC

Next row (RS) Cast on 39 sts, then k1, [p1, k1] 19 times across these sts, work chart pat to last 39 sts, rib 39. Pm each end of last row to mark beg of sleeve extensions. Work even on 179 (189, 199, 209) sts in this way until piece measures 11½ (12, 12½, 13)"/29 (30.5, 32, 33)cm from markers. Bind off all sts.

FRONT

Work as for back until armhole measures 9½ (10, 10½, 11)"/24 (25.5, 26.5, 28)cm from the markers. Mark the center 11 (11, 13, 13) sts on last WS row.

Neck shaping

Next row (RS) Work to marker, join a 2nd ball of yarn and bind off center 11 (11, 13, 13) sts, work to end. Working both sides at once, bind off 3 sts from each neck edge twice, 2 sts once, then 1 st once—75 (80, 84, 89) sts rem each side. Bind off rem sts each side for shoulders.

FINISHING

Sew side and shoulder seams, being sure to sew sleeve cuffs from WS (for sleeve turn back). Tack sleeve in place at underarm and at shoulder seam.

COLLAR

With size 8 (5mm) circular needle, pick up and k 68 (68, 72, 72) sts evenly around neck edge. Join and pm to mark beg of rnds.

Inc rnd 1 *K1, (p1, k1) in next st, p1, (k1, p1) in next st; rep from * around—102 (102, 108, 108) sts. Working in k1, p1 rib, work 6 rnds, change to shorter size 9 (5.5mm) circular needle, work 6 rnds. Cont in this way, working 6 rnds with each consecutive circular needle, finishing with size 13 (9mm). Bind off in rib. ∎

Cabled Poncho

Take loungewear to the next level. Norah Gaughan's sumptuous oversized poncho is worked side to side in a rib-and-cable pattern.

SIZES

Sized for Small/Large, X-Large/1X and shown in size Small/Large.

KNITTED MEASUREMENTS

Width at one lower edge 40 (45)"/101.5 (114)cm
Length 27 (29¾)"/68.5 (75)cm

MATERIALS

• 12 (15) 1¾oz/50g balls (each approx 130yd/119m) of Berroco *Blackstone Tweed* (wool/mohair/angora) in #2601 clover honey (4) *

• One each sizes 5 and 7 (3.75 and 4.5mm) circular needle, 40"/100cm long, OR SIZE TO OBTAIN GAUGE

• Size 5 (3.75mm) circular needle, 24"/60cm long (for ribbed collar)

• Cable needle (cn)

• Stitch markers

GAUGE

20 sts and 27 rows = 4"/10cm over cable chart pat using larger needle.
TAKE TIME TO CHECK GAUGE.

** Yarn used in original pattern is no
longer available and is listed on page 190.*

NOTES

1) Poncho is worked in one piece (see schematic for direction of knitting) with center line inc's, an opening for neck, then center line dec's.
2) The center line inc's/dec's form the placement of the poncho along the shoulders (see photo).

STITCH GLOSSARY

6-st RC Sl 3 sts to cn and hold to back, k3, k3 from cn.
6-st LC Sl 3 sts to cn and hold to front, k3, k3 from cn.

PONCHO

Beg with the left side opening edge, with longer size 5 (3.75mm) needle, cast on 143 sts.
Row 1 (WS) P1, *k1, p1; rep from * to end.
Cont in k1, p1 rib for 3 rows more. Change to size 7 (4.5mm) circular needle.
Next row (WS) Cast on 3 sts, purl to end.

Beg cable chart

Row 1 (RS) Cast on 3 sts, and working over these 3 sts, beg with chart A row 1 st 1 and work to the rep line (3 sts), work the 13-st rep 5 times (65 sts), work to end of chart A (5 sts), pm, k3, pm, beg with chart B row 1 st 1 and work to the rep line (2 sts), work the 13-st rep 5 times (65 sts), work to end of chart B (6 sts)—149 sts (73 sts each side of center 3 sts).

Row 2 Work even foll row 2 of each established chart with center 3 sts worked as p3 on this and every WS row.

Cont to work 8-row reps of chart A and chart B, AT SAME TIME work increase rows as foll:

*Next (inc) row (RS) Work chart A to marker, M1 in chart pat, sl marker (sm), k3, sm, M1 in chart pat, work chart B to end—2 sts inc'd.

Next row (WS) Work even.

Next (inc) row (RS) Work chart A to marker, M1 in chart pat, sm, k3, sm, M1 in chart pat, work chart B to end—2 sts inc'd.

Next (inc) row (WS) Work chart B to marker, M1 in chart pat, sm, p3, sm, M1 in chart pat, work chart A to end—2 sts inc'd.

Rep from * 20 (24) times more, working increased sts in chart pats—275 (299) sts.

Size Small/Large only

Next (inc) row (RS) Work chart A to marker, M1 in chart pat, sm, k3, sm, M1 in chart pat, work chart B to end.

Next row (WS) Work even.

Next (inc) row (RS) Work chart A to marker, M1 in

chart pat, sm, k3, sm, M1 in chart pat, work chart B to end—279 sts.

Size X-Large/1X only

Next row (RS) Work even. There are 138 (151) sts and 10 (11) cable reps on EACH side of center 3 sts—279 (305) sts.

Neck opening

Next row (WS) Work even to marker, sm, p2, join a 2nd ball of yarn and M1p, p1, sm, work to end. Cont to work even on 140 (153) sts each side for a total of 14"/35.5cm from beg of opening, end with a WS row.

Rejoin two halves

Next row (RS) Work to first marker, k1, then k last st of first side tog with first st of 2nd side, work to end. Drop the markers and thread the center line 3 k sts with a safety pin or removable st marker and move this marker up every row—279 (305) sts.

Next row (WS) Work even on all sts.

Dec row 1 (RS) Work chart A pat to 1 st before the 3 marked sts, then k2tog, k1, ssk, work chart B pat to end.

Row 2 Work even.

Row 3 Rep dec row 1.

Dec row 4 (WS) Work chart B pat to 1 st before the 3 marked sts, p2tog tbl, p1, p2tog, work chart A pat to end.

Rep rows 1–4 for 20 (24) times more, then rep row 1 once (0 times) more. Work 1 row even. There are 70 sts and a total of 5 cable reps each side once again, end with a RS row on the 149 sts.

Change to longer size 5 (3.75mm) needle.

Next row (WS) Bind off 3 sts, purl to end.

Next row (RS) Bind off 3 sts, work in k1, p1 rib to end.

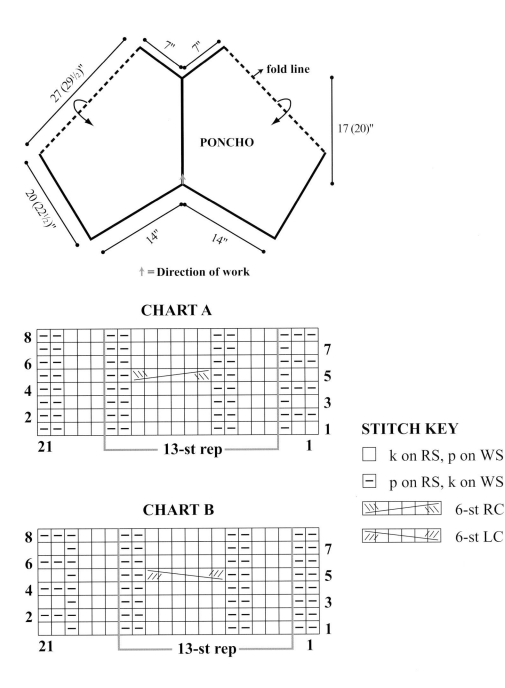

PONCHO

7" 7"

27 (29½)"

fold line

17 (20)"

20 (22½)"

14" 14"

↑ = **Direction of work**

CHART A

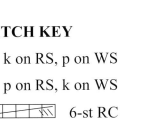

8
6
4
2

7
5
3
1

21   13-st rep   1

STITCH KEY

☐   k on RS, p on WS

▬   p on RS, k on WS

  6-st RC

  6-st LC

CHART B

8
6
4
2

7
5
3
1

21   13-st rep   1

Cont in k1, p1 rib for 3 rows more.

Bind off in rib.

FINISHING

Fold 3 sts along each side edge of the poncho to the WS and sew in place, forming a hem facing.

Collar

With RS facing and shorter size 5 (3.75mm) needle, pick up and k 128 sts evenly spaced around neck opening. Join and work in k1, p1 rib for 1"/2.5cm. Knit 1 rnd. Work in k2, p2 rib for 1¾"/4.5cm. Knit 1 rnd. Work in k1, p1 rib for 1"/2.5cm more. Bind off loosely in rib. ■

Cable-Edged Cardi

The cabled collar treatment of Rosemary Drysdale's tie-front cardi attaches intermittently to the sand-stitch body for a unique tied look.

SIZES

Sized for Small, Medium, Large, 1X, 2X, 3X and shown in size Medium.

KNITTED MEASUREMENTS

Bust (closed) 34 (38, 42, 46, 50, 54)"/86 (96.5, 106.5, 117, 127, 137)cm

Length 24½ (25½, 26, 27, 27½, 28)"/62.5 (64.5, 66, 68.5, 70, 71)cm

Upper arm 9 (10, 11, 12, 13, 14)"/23 (25.5, 28, 30.5, 33, 35.5)cm

MATERIALS

• 9 (10, 11, 12, 13, 14) 1¾oz/50g balls (each approx 162yd/148m) of S. Charles Collezione/Tahki•Stacy Charles *Eclipse* (cotton/polyester/nylon) in #01 silver (4)

• One pair size 7 (4.5mm) needles OR SIZE TO OBTAIN GAUGE

• Cable needle (cn) and stitch markers

GAUGE

19 sts and 25 rows = 4"/10cm over sand st using size 7 (4.5mm) needles.
TAKE TIME TO CHECK GAUGE.

SAND STITCH

(over an odd number of sts)
Row 1 (RS) K1, *p1, k1; rep from * to end.

Rows 2 and 4 Purl.

Row 3 P1, *k1, p1; rep from * to end.

Rep rows 1–4 for sand st.

BACK

Cast on 77 (85, 95, 105, 115, 123) sts. Work sand st for 14½ (15, 15, 15½, 15½, 15½)"/37 (38, 38, 39.5, 39.5, 39.5)cm.

Sleeve shaping

Inc 1 st each side on next row, then every other row 3 times more. Cast on 2 sts at beg of next 8 rows, 3 sts at beg of next 4 rows, 4 (4, 4, 5, 5, 5) sts at beg of next 2 rows, 5 sts at beg of next 2 rows, 6 (6, 6, 7, 7, 7) sts at beg of next 2 rows and 6 (7, 7, 7, 7, 7) sts at beg of next 2 rows—155 (165, 175, 189, 199, 207) sts. Place a marker at beg of last row. Work even until piece measures 4½ (5, 5½, 6, 6½, 7)"/11.5 (12.5, 14, 15, 16.5, 17.5)cm above marker.

Shoulder shaping

Bind off 20 (22, 23, 26, 27, 28) sts at beg of next of next 4 rows, 21 (22, 24, 25, 27, 29) sts at beg of next 2 rows. Bind off rem 33 (33, 35, 35, 37, 37) sts for back neck.

LEFT FRONT

Cast on 47 (51, 55, 61, 65, 71) sts. Work in sand st until same length as back to sleeve shaping. Work sleeve shaping at side edge (beg of RS rows) as for back, AT SAME TIME, when piece measures 15½ (16, 16½, 17, 17½, 17½)"/39.5 (40.5, 42, 43, 44.5, 44.5)cm from beg, work as foll:

Neck shaping

Dec 1 st at neck edge (end of RS rows) on next row, then every other row 24 (24, 24, 25, 25, 27) times more. Work even on rem 61 (66, 70, 77, 81, 85) sts until same length as back to shoulder. Shape shoulder at side edge as for back.

RIGHT FRONT

Work to correspond to left front, reversing all shaping.

FINISHING

Block pieces lightly to measurements. Sew shoulder and top of sleeve seams. Sew side and under sleeve seams.

Cable tie/border

Cast on 12 sts. Work in sand st for 13"/33cm. Place a marker each end of row for tie.

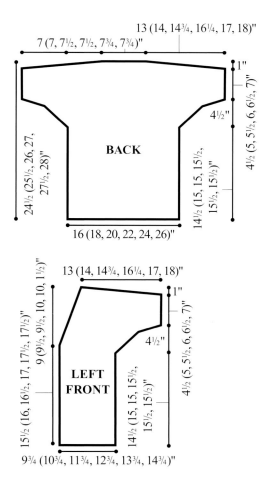

Beg cable border

Row 1 (RS) Knit.

Row 2 and all WS rows Purl.

Row 3 Slip 6 sts to cn and hold to front, k6, k6 from cn.

Rows 5, 7, 9, and 11 Knit.

Row 12 Purl.

Rep rows 1–12 until cable border fits along left front, back, and right front neck. At this point, lay border around neck edge and adjust length if necessary. Place marker at each end of last row. Work in sand st for 13"/33cm from last marker for tie. Bind off sts knitwise. Tack cable border around neck edge, joining 1 st of border to neck edge approx every 1"/2.5cm. ■

Double-Breasted Cardi

Ornamental yet as comfortable as well-worn denim, Yoko Hatta's double-breasted jacket is decorated with a brass-buttoned placket, epaulets, and a military collar.

SIZES

Sized for X-Small, Small/Medium, Large, X-Large, XX-Large and shown in size Small/Medium.

KNITTED MEASUREMENTS

Bust 32 (36, 42, 46, 50)"/81 (91.5, 106.5, 117, 127)cm

Length 27½ (28, 28½, 29, 29½)"/70 (71, 72.5, 73.5, 75)cm

Upper arm 14 (15, 16, 17, 18)"/35.5 (38, 40.5, 43, 45.5)cm

MATERIALS

• 13 (14, 17, 18, 20) 1¾oz/50g hanks (each approx 96yd/88m) of Debbie Bliss/KFI *Donegal Luxury Tweed Aran* (wool/angora) in #09 denim ◀4▶

• One pair each sizes 6 and 7 (4 and 4.5mm) needles OR SIZE TO OBTAIN GAUGE

• 16¾"/19mm buttons

• Stitch markers

• Cable needle (cn)

GAUGE

18 sts and 27 rows = 4"/10cm over double seed st using larger needles.
TAKE TIME TO CHECK GAUGE.

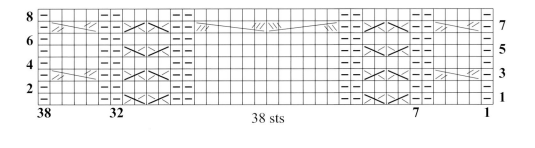

Stitch Key

☐ k on RS, p on WS   ⬚ 2-st RC   ⬚ 4-st LC   ⬚ 6-st LC

⊟ p on RS, k on WS   ⬚ 2-st LC   ⬚ 6-st RC

STITCH GLOSSARY

2-st RC Sl 1 st to cn, hold to *back*, k1, k1 from cn.

2-st LC Sl 1 st to cn, hold to *front*, k1, k1 from cn.

4-st LC Sl 2 sts to cn, hold to *front*, k2, k2 from cn.

6-st RC Sl 3 sts to cn, hold to *back*, k3, k3 from cn.

6-st LC Sl 3 sts to cn, hold to *front*, k3, k3 from cn.

DOUBLE SEED STITCH

(over an odd number of sts)

Row 1 K1, *p1, k1; rep from * to end.

Row 2 P1, *k1, p1; rep from * to end.

Row 3 P1, *k1, p1; rep from * to end.

Row 4 K1, *p1, k1; rep from * to end.

Rep rows 1–4 for double seed st.

DOUBLE SEED STITCH

(over an even number of sts)

Row 1 *P1, k1; rep from * to end.

Row 2 *K1, p1; rep from * to end.

Row 3 *K1, p1; rep from * to end.

Row 4 *P1, k1; rep from * to end.

Rep rows 1–4 for double seed st.

BACK

With smaller needles, cast on 80 (90, 105, 115, 125) sts. Work in garter st (k every row) until piece measures 2"/5cm from beg.

Next row (inc WS) Inc 21 (21, 16, 16, 16) sts evenly across row—101 (111, 121, 131, 141) sts. Change to larger needles.

Beg chart

Row 1 (RS) Work 5 (10, 15, 20, 25) sts in double seed st, work chart over 38 sts, work 15 sts in double seed st, work chart over 38 sts, work 5 (10, 15, 20, 25) sts in double seed st. Cont in pats as established until piece measures 20½"/52 cm from beg, end with a WS row.

Armhole shaping

Bind off 3 sts at beg of next 2 rows.

Dec 2 sts each side of next row, then dec 1 st each side every other row 4 (4, 4, 6, 8) times, then every 4th row 1 (1, 2, 3, 3) times—81 (91, 99, 103, 109) sts. Work even until armhole measures 6 (6½, 7, 7½, 8)"/15 (16.5, 18, 19, 20.5)cm, end with a WS row. Place marker (pm) to mark center 27 sts.

Neck shaping

Next row (RS) Work to center marked sts, join 2nd ball of yarn and bind off center 27 sts, work to end. Working both sides at once, bind off 1 st from each neck edge once, then 2 sts from each neck edge twice. Bind off rem 22 (27, 31, 33, 36) sts each side.

LEFT FRONT

With smaller needles, cast on 29 (34, 41, 46, 51) sts. Work in garter st (k every row) until piece measures 2"/5cm from beg.

Next row (inc WS) Inc 8 (8, 6, 6, 6) sts evenly across row—37 (42, 47, 52, 57) sts. Change to larger needles.

Beg chart

Row 1 (RS) Work 5 (10, 15, 20, 25) sts in double seed st, work sts 1–32 of chart. Cont in pats as established until piece measures same length as back to armhole.

Armhole shaping

Work armhole shaping at side edge (beg of RS rows) as for back—27 (32, 36, 38, 41) sts. Work even until armhole measures 3½ (4, 4½, 5, 5½)"/9 (10, 11.5, 12.5, 14)cm, end with a RS row.

Neck shaping

Dec 1 st at beg (neck edge) of next row, then dec 1 st every 4th row 3 times, then every 6th row once— 22 (27, 31, 33, 36) sts. Work even until armhole measures same as back to shoulder. Bind off.

Button band

With smaller needles, cast on 23 sts. Work in garter st until piece measures same as left front to neck

shaping. Bind off. Place marker (pm) between 11th and 12th sts of last row for collar.

Sew button band to left front. Pm on button band for 7 buttons, the first one 1¾"/4.5cm from lower edge, the last one ½"/1cm from neck edge, and the rem 5 spaced evenly between.

RIGHT FRONT

With smaller needles, cast on 29 (34, 41, 46, 51) sts. Work in garter st until piece measures 2"/5cm from beg.

Next row (inc WS) Inc 8 (8, 6, 6, 6) sts evenly across row—37 (42, 47, 52, 57) sts. Change to larger needles.

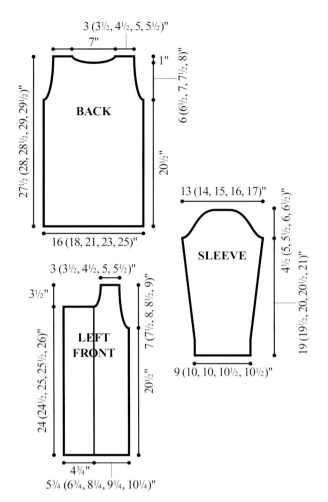

BACK

3 (3½, 4½, 5, 5½)"
7"
1"
6 (6½, 7, 7½, 8)"
27½ (28, 28½, 29, 29½)"
20½"
16 (18, 21, 23, 25)"

SLEEVE

13 (14, 15, 16, 17)"
4½ (5, 5½, 6, 6½)"
19 (19½, 20, 20½, 21)"
9 (10, 10, 10½, 10½)"

LEFT FRONT

3 (3½, 4½, 5, 5½)"
3½"
7 (7½, 8, 8½, 9)"
24 (24½, 25, 25½, 26)"
20½"
4¾"
5¾ (6¾, 8¼, 9¼, 10¼)"

Beg chart

Row 1 (RS) Work sts 7–38 of chart, work 5 (10, 15, 20, 25) sts in double seed st.

Complete to correspond to left front, reversing all shaping by binding off for armhole at beg of WS rows and working neck shaping at end of RS rows.

Buttonhole band

With smaller needles, cast on 23 sts. Work in garter st until piece measures same as right front to neck shaping, AT SAME TIME, work buttonhole row opposite button markers as foll:

Buttonhole row (RS) K3, k2tog, yo, k12, k2tog, yo, k4.

Bind off. Place marker (pm) between 11th and 12th sts of last row for collar.

Sew buttonhole band to right front.

SLEEVES

With smaller needles, cast on 44 (50, 50, 52, 52) sts. Work in garter st until piece measures 2½"/6.5cm from beg.

Next row (inc WS) Inc 4 sts evenly across row—48 (54, 54, 56, 56) sts. Change to larger needles.

Beg chart

Row 1 (RS) Work 11 (14, 14, 15, 15) sts in double seed st, work sts 7–32 of chart, work 11 (14, 14, 15, 15) sts in double seed st. Cont in pats as established, AT SAME TIME, inc 1 st each side every 14th (14th, 10th, 10th, 10th) row 4 (4, 11, 7, 4) times, then every 10th (10th, 0, 8th, 8th) row 5 (5, 0, 5, 10) times, working inc'd sts into double

seed st—66 (72, 76, 80, 84) sts. Work even until piece measures 19 (19½, 20, 20½, 21)"/48 (49.5, 51, 52, 53.5)cm from beg, end with a WS row.

Cap shaping

Bind off 3 sts at beg of next 2 rows, then 2 sts at beg of next 2 rows. Dec 1 st each side every other row 9 (11, 12, 14, 16) times—38 (40, 42, 42, 42) sts. Bind off 2 sts at beg of next 4 rows. Bind off 3 sts at beg of next 2 rows, then 4 sts at beg of next 2 rows. Bind off rem 16 (18, 20, 20, 20) sts.

FINISHING

Sew shoulder seams. Set in sleeves. Sew side and sleeve seams. Sew buttons to left front button band to correspond to buttonholes.

Collar

With smaller needles and WS of body facing, pick up and k 31 sts from left front button band marker to left shoulder, 31 (35, 37, 37, 41) sts across back neck, 31 sts from right shoulder to right front button band marker—93 (97, 99, 99, 103) sts. Work in garter st until collar measures 2½"/6.5cm. Change to larger needles, cont in garter st until collar measures 5"/12.5cm. Bind off.

Epaulet (make 2)

With smaller needles, cast on 8 sts. Work in garter st until piece measures 4"/10cm.

Next (buttonhole) row (RS) K3, k2tog, yo, k3.

Cont in garter st until piece measures 5"/12.5cm. Bind off.

Sew cast-on edge of epaulet to base of collar over shoulder seam. Sew button to top of shoulder to correspond to buttonhole. ■

Reindeer Capelet

Little Red meets Nordic chic. Yoko Hatta's reindeer capelet is a great project for a stranded colorwork beginner. It's worked in two halves that are joined before the side edges are picked up and ribbed.

SIZES

Sized for Small, Medium, Large, 1X, 2X, 3X and shown in size Small.

KNITTED MEASUREMENTS

Width of piece after side ribbed edges 20¾ (20¾, 20¾, 25, 25, 25)"/52.5 (52.5, 52.5, 63.5, 63.5, 63.5)cm
Finished length from end to end 49 (50, 51, 52, 53, 54)"/124 (127, 129, 132, 134, 137)cm

MATERIALS

• 5 (5, 5, 6, 6, 6) 3½oz/100g skeins (each approx 138yd/125m) of Manos del Uruguay/Fairmount Fibers *Wool Clasica* (wool) in #49 henna (MC) 🔲4

• 1 skein in #48 cherry (CC)

• One pair each sizes 8 and 9 (5 and 5.5mm) needles OR SIZE TO OBTAIN GAUGE

• Size 8 (5mm) circular needle, 40"/100cm long

• G-6 (4mm) crochet hook (for button loop)

• Stitch holders

• One 1⅜"/34mm button

GAUGE

16 sts and 20 rows = 4"/10cm over St st using size 9 (5.5mm) needles.
TAKE TIME TO CHECK GAUGE.

K2, P2 RIB

(multiple of 4 sts)
Row 1 (RS) K3, *p2, k2; rep from *, end k3.
Row 2 K the knit sts and p the purl sts.
Rep row 2 for k2, p2 rib.

LEFT HALF

With smaller needles and MC, cast on 76 (76, 76, 96, 96, 96) sts. Work in k2, p2 rib for 1"/2.5cm, dec 1 (1, 1, 3, 3, 3) sts on last row—75 (75, 75, 93, 93, 93) sts. Change to larger needles. Work in St st as foll: Work 2 rows with MC.

Beg reindeer chart 1
Row 1 (RS) Work first 2 sts of chart, work 18-st rep 4 (4, 4, 5, 5, 5) times, work last st of chart. Cont in pat as established through row 34, dec 0 (0, 0, 1, 1, 1) st on last row—75 (75, 75, 92, 92, 92) sts.
Row 35 (RS) Rep first 8 sts (outlined in green) 9 (9, 9, 11, 11, 11) times, then work next 3 (3, 3, 4, 4, 4) sts. Cont in pat as established through row 37. Cont with MC only until piece measures 24½ (25, 25½, 26, 26½, 27)"/62 (63.5, 64.5, 66, 67, 68.5)cm from beg. Place sts on a holder.

RIGHT HALF

Work as for left half, but work chart 2 instead of chart 1.

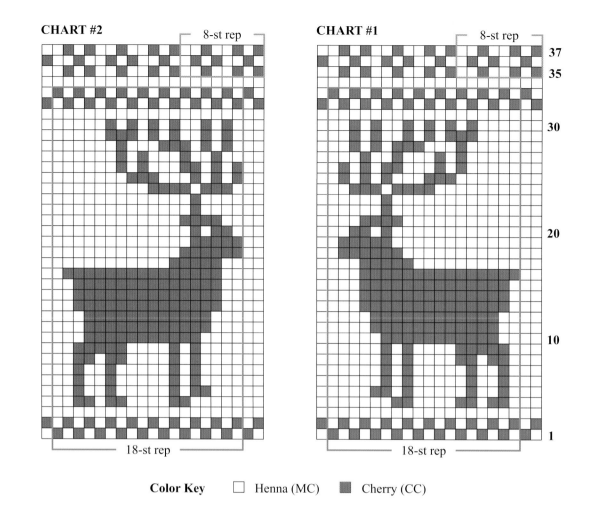

CHART #2

8-st rep

CHART #1

8-st rep

37
35
30
20
10
1

18-st rep

18-st rep

Color Key ☐ Henna (MC) ■ Cherry (CC)

FINISHING

Block pieces to measurements. Join sts from both pieces using kitchener st or 3-needle bind off.

Side edging

With RS facing, circular needle and MC, pick up and k 208 (212, 216, 220, 224, 228) sts evenly along one long side of piece. Work in k2, p2 rib for 1"/2.5cm. Bind off loosely in rib. Work in same way along other side.

Sew button to left half at 8½"/21.5cm from lower edge. Work button loop on right half opposite button as foll: with crochet hook, join MC into edge of bind-off row and ch 9–10 (or size to fit button), skip 4 sts and join with sl st into next st. Fasten off and secure. ■

Reverse Stripe Cowl Neck

Everything from the deep ribbed cowl to the hip-hugging lower border is exaggerated on Mari Lynn Patrick's dramatic oversized pullover.

SIZES

Sized for Small/Medium, Large/X-Large, XX-Large and shown in size Small/Medium.

KNITTED MEASUREMENTS

Bust 49 (51, 53)"/124.5 (129.5, 134.5)cm

Length 28 (29, 30)"/71 (73.5, 76)cm

Upper arm 18 (19¼, 20½)"/45.5 (49, 52)cm

MATERIALS

• 8 (9, 10) 1¾oz/50g balls (each approx 96yd/88m) of Debbie Bliss/KFI *Donegal Luxury Tweed Aran* (wool/angora) each in #10 slate grey (A) and #15 charcoal grey (B) (4)

• 8 (9, 10) 1¾oz/50g balls (each approx 125yd/114m) of Debbie Bliss/KFI *Cashmerino DK* (wool/microfibre/cashmere) in #1 black (C) (3)

• One pair each sizes 8 and 11 (5 and 8mm) needles OR SIZE TO OBTAIN GAUGES

• Sizes 7 and 8 (4.5 and 5mm) circular needle, each 24"/60cm long

• Stitch markers

GAUGES

13 sts and 16 rows = 4"/10cm over St st using 1 strand A and B held tog and size 11 (8mm) needles. 20 sts and 20 rows = 4"/10cm over k1, p1 rib using 2 strands C held tog and size 8 (5mm) needles. TAKE TIME TO CHECK GAUGES.

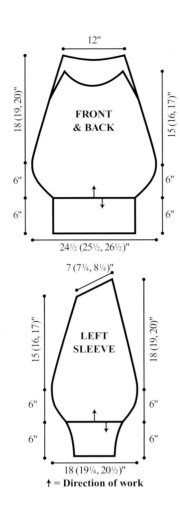

12"

18 (19, 20)"   15 (16, 17)"

FRONT & BACK

6"   6"

6"   6"

24½ (25½, 26½)"

7 (7¾, 8¼)"

15 (16, 17)"   18 (19, 20)"

LEFT SLEEVE

6"   6"

6"   6"

18 (19¼, 20½)"

↑ = Direction of work

BACK

Note Ribbed edges in double strand C are picked up and worked after finishing main pieces.

With 2 strands A and size 11 (8mm) needles, cast on 79 (83, 87) sts.

Row 1 (RS) With A, purl.

Row 2 With B, knit.

Row 3 With B, purl.

Row 4 With A, knit. Rep rows 1–4 for tweed stripes pat until piece measures 6"/15cm from beg, end with a purl row. Place markers each side of last row to mark for beg of armholes.

Raglan armhole shaping

Dec row 1 (WS) K1, SKP, k to the last 3 sts, k2tog, k1.

Work 3 rows even. Rep the last 4 rows 15 times more—47 (51, 55) sts.

Dec row 2 (WS) K1, SK2P, k to the last 4 sts, k3tog, k1. Rep dec row 2 every 4th row 1 (2, 3) times more—39 sts. Work 3 rows even. Bind off.

FRONT

Work as for the back to the raglan armhole.

Raglan armhole shaping

Dec row 1 (WS) K1, SKP, k to last 3 sts, k2tog, k1. Work 3 rows even. Rep last 4 rows 11 times more—55 (59, 63) sts.

Dec row 2 (WS) K1, SK2P, k to last 4 sts, k3tog, k1. Rep dec row 2 every 4th row 2 (3, 4) times more, AT SAME TIME, when armhole measures 13¾ (14¾, 15¾)"/35 (37.5, 40)cm from markers, shape neck as foll:

Neck shaping

Next row (RS) Bind off center 15 sts. Then, working both sides at once, bind off 3 sts from each neck edge 4 times. After all shaping is completed, fasten off the 2 rem sts each side of neck.

LEFT SLEEVE

With 2 strands of A, cast on 59 (63, 67) sts. Work in stripe pat as for back for 6"/15cm, end with a purl row. Place markers each side of last row to mark for beg of armholes.

Raglan cap shaping

Dec row 1 (WS) Work as for back. Work 3 rows even. Rep last 4 rows 14 (15, 16) times more—29 (31, 33) sts.

Top of cap shaping

Bind off 4 sts at beg of the next 5 WS rows, AT SAME TIME, dec 2 sts at beg of every 4th row (by k1, S2KP) 3 times more. Bind off rem 3 (5, 7) sts.

RIGHT SLEEVE

Work same as for left sleeve, reversing shaping at top of cap by binding off 4 sts at beg of RS rows and dec 2 sts every 4th row 3 times by K3tog, k1 at end of RS rows.

Sleeve cuff trim

With size 8 (5mm) needles and 2 strands C held tog, pick up and k 57 (61, 65) sts from RS of sleeve cuff. Work in k1, p1 rib for 6"/15cm. Bind off firmly in rib.

Lower edge trim

With size 8 (5mm) needles and 2 strands C held tog, pick up and k 77 (81, 85) sts from RS of lower back edge. Work in k1, p1 rib for 6"/15cm. Bind off firmly in rib. Work front lower edge in same way.

FINISHING

Sew raglan sleeves into armholes. Sew side and sleeve seams.

Collar

With larger circular needle and 2 strands C, from RS, pick up and k 122 (126, 130) sts evenly around entire neck edge. Join and pm to mark beg of rnd. Work in rnds of k1, p1 rib for 2½"/6.5cm. Change to smaller circular needle and cont in rib for 6"/12.5cm more. Bind off firmly in rib. ∎

Red Striped Pullover

Ethereal yet fiery, Wayne's red-hot take on the classic boatneck pullover is a casual delight. It's striped with alternating wide mohair stripes and narrow smooth wool stripes.

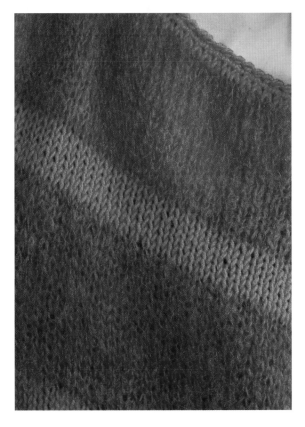

SIZES

Sized for Small, Medium, Large, X-Large, XX-Large and shown in size Small.

KNITTED MEASUREMENTS

Bust 41 (45, 49, 52, 56)"/104 (114, 124.5, 132, 142)cm
Length 25½ (25½, 26, 26½, 26½)"/64.5 (64.5, 66, 67, 67)cm
Upper arm 15 (16, 17, 18, 19)"/38 (40.5, 43, 45.5, 48)cm

MATERIALS

• 3 (3, 3, 4, 4) 1¾oz/50g hanks (each approx 93yd/85m) of Kollåge *Fantastic* (wool) in #7514 vixen red (A) 🔘4

• 5 (5, 6, 6, 7) 1¾oz/50g hanks (each approx 115yd/105m) of Kollåge *Whimsy* (mohair/wool/nylon) in #7006 indian red (B) 🔘4

• One pair each sizes 10 and 11 (6 and 8mm) needles OR SIZE TO OBTAIN GAUGE

• Stitch markers

GAUGE

12½ sts and 16 rows = 4"/10cm over St st using larger needles and A or B.
TAKE TIME TO CHECK GAUGE.

STRIPE PATTERN

Work in St st in foll stripes: *4½"/11.5cm (18 rows) B, 1½"/4cm (6 rows) A; rep from * for stripe pat.

BACK

With smaller needles and A, cast on 66 (70, 78, 82, 90) sts. Work in k2, p2 rib for 1 (1½, 2, 2½, 2½)"/4 (4, 5, 6.5, 6.5)cm, dec 2 (0, 2, 0, 2) sts across last WS row—64 (70, 76, 82, 88) sts.

Change to larger needles. Work in stripe pat until 24 rows of pat have been worked 3 times, then work 20 rows in pat once more, ending with 2 rows A (92 rows in total)—piece measures approx 24½ (24½ 25, 25½, 25½)"/62 (62, 63.5, 64.5, 64.5)cm from beg.

Shoulder and neck shaping

Cont with A, bind off 8 (9, 10, 11, 13) sts at beg of next 2 rows, 8 (9, 11, 12, 13) sts at beg of next 2 rows, AT THE SAME TIME, bind off center 26 (28, 28, 30, 30) sts for neck and, working both sides at once, bind off 3 sts from each neck edge once.

FRONT

Work same as back.

SLEEVES

With smaller needles and A, cast on 34 sts. Work in k2, p2 rib for 1½ (1½, 1½, 2, 2)"/4 (4, 4, 5, 5)cm, inc 1 (0, 1, 0, 0) st on last WS row—35 (34, 35, 34, 34) sts. Change to larger needles. Work in stripe pat, inc 1 st each side every 10th (6th, 6th, 4th, 4th) row 6 (1, 5, 2, 8) times, every 0 (8th, 8th, 6th, 6th) row 0 (7, 4, 9, 5) times—47 (50, 53, 56, 60) sts. Work even until piece measures 18 (18, 18, 18½, 18½)"/45.5 (45.5, 45.5, 47, 47)cm from beg, end with 18 rows B. Bind off.

FINISHING

Block pieces lightly to measurements. Sew shoulder seams. Place markers 7½ (8, 8½, 9, 9½)"/19 (20.5, 21.5, 23, 24)cm down from shoulder seams on

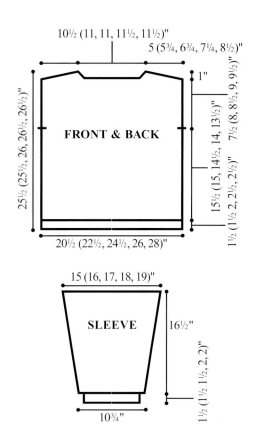

front and back for armholes. Sew top of sleeves to front and back between markers. Sew side and sleeve seams.

Neckband

With RS facing, crochet hook and A, work 1 rnd sc evenly around neck edge, then work 1 rnd backwards sc (from left to right) in each sc. Fasten off. ∎

Striped Raglan Tee

Loren Cherensky uses citrusy striping and raglan shaping to turn a basic short-sleeve top into a bona fide head turner.

SIZES

Sized for X-Small, Small, Medium, Large, 1X, 2X and shown in size Small.

KNITTED MEASUREMENTS

Bust 33 (37, 41, 45, 49, 53)"/84 (94, 104, 114, 124.5, 134.5)cm

Length 20 (20¾, 21½, 22½, 23½, 24½)"/51 (52.5, 54.5, 57, 59.5, 62)cm

Upper arm 12½ (13¼, 14, 15, 15½, 16½)"/32 (33.5, 35.5, 39.5, 42)cm

MATERIALS

• 3 (3, 3, 4, 4, 5) 4oz/113g hanks (each approx 200yd/183m) of Prism *Windward* (rayon/cotton) each in #204 orange (MC) and #305 yellow (CC) 〖4〗

• One pair size 6 (4mm) needles OR SIZE TO OBTAIN GAUGE

• Size 6 (4mm) circular needle, 32"/80cm long

• One size E-4 (3.5mm) crochet hook

• Stitch holders and markers

GAUGE

20 sts and 28 rows = 4"/10cm over St st using size 6 (4mm) needles.

TAKE TIME TO CHECK GAUGE.

* Yarn used in original pattern is no longer available and is listed on page 190.

BACK

With MC and straight needles, cast on 70 (80, 90, 100, 110, 120) sts. Work in k1, p1 rib for 2"/5cm, end with a WS row and inc 6 sts evenly spaced across this row—76 (86, 96, 106, 116, 126) sts.

Beg stripe pattern

Rows 1–6 Work in St st with CC.

Rows 7–12 Work in St st with MC. Rep rows 1–12 for stripe pat, AT SAME TIME, when 8 rows are complete, work as foll:

Inc row (RS) K1, M1, k to last st, M1, k1. Rep inc row every 8th row twice more—82 (92, 102, 112, 122, 132) sts. Work even until a total of 70 (72, 74, 76, 78, 82) rows of stripe pat have been worked, end with a WS row. Place sts on holder.

FRONT

Work same as for back.

SLEEVES (make 2)

With MC and straight needles, cast on 46 (50, 54, 58, 62, 66) sts. Work in k1, p1 rib for 1½"/4cm, inc 16 sts on the last WS row—62 (66, 70, 74, 78, 82) sts. Work 10 (12, 14, 16, 18, 22) rows in stripe pat, end with a WS row. Place sts on holder.

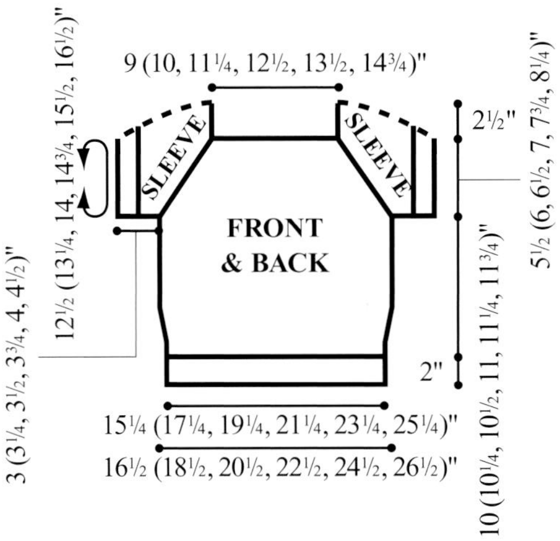
9 (10, 11¼, 12½, 13½, 14¾)"
12½ (13¼, 14, 14¾, 15½, 16½)"
SLEEVE
SLEEVE
FRONT & BACK
2½"
5½ (6, 6½, 7, 7¾, 8¼)"
3 (3¼, 3½, 3¾, 4, 4½)"
2"
10 (10¼, 10½, 11, 11¼, 11¾)"
15¼ (17¼, 19¼, 21¼, 23¼, 25¼)"
16½ (18½, 20½, 22½, 24½, 26½)"

YOKE

Joining rnd With circular needle and cont in stripe pat as established, k 62 (66, 70, 74, 78, 82) sts of left sleeve, pm, k 82 (92, 102, 112, 122, 132) sts of front, pm, k 62 (66, 70, 74, 78, 82) sts of right sleeve, pm, k 82 (92, 102, 112, 122, 132) sts of back, place different-colored marker for beg of rnd—288 (316, 344, 372, 400, 428) sts.

Dec rnd *SKP, work to 2 sts before marker, k2tog, slip marker; rep from * 3 times more—8 sts dec'd.

Rep dec rnd every other rnd 18 (20, 22, 24, 26, 28) times—136 (148, 160, 172, 184, 196) sts; 44 (50, 56, 62, 68, 74) sts each for front and back, 24 sts for each sleeve.

Work 1 rnd even, end with 6 rows MC (CC, MC, CC, MC, CC). Bind off.

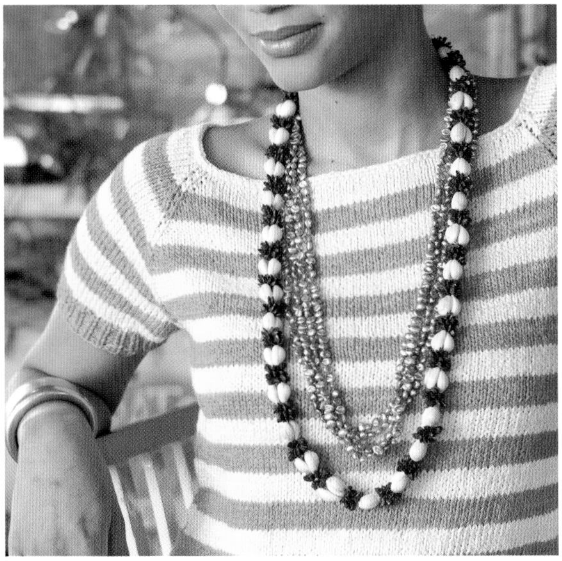

FINISHING

Block to finished measurements. Sew side and sleeve seams.

With crochet hook and MC (CC, MC, CC, MC, CC), work 1 rnd of sc around neck opening. ■

Striped Back Top

This boxy pullover marries two classic Twinkle looks: folksy flair (in the front) and sporty stripes (in the back). Large-scale ribbing ties it together.

SIZES

Sized for Small, Medium, Large and shown in size Small.

KNITTED MEASUREMENTS

Bust 40 (44, 48)"/101.5 (111.5, 122)cm

Length 20½ (23, 25)"/52 (58.5, 63.5)cm

MATERIALS

• 3 (4, 4) 8⅚oz/250g hanks (each approx 123yd/112m) of Cascade Yarns *Magnum* (wool) in #9549 koala bear (MC)

• 1 (1, 2) hanks in #8393 navy (CC) (6) *

• One pair each sizes 15, 17, and 19 (10, 12.75, 15mm) needles OR SIZE TO OBTAIN GAUGES

• Two 1½"/38mm buttons

GAUGES

For back

6 sts and 9 rows = 4"/10cm over St st using size 19 (15mm) needles.

For front

9 sts and 12 rows = 4"/10cm over St st using size 15 (10mm) needles.

TAKE TIME TO CHECK GAUGES.

* Yarn used in original pattern is no longer available and is listed on page 190.

NOTES

1) There are selvage sts each side on back and front. Because of the difference in gauges, there is a ½ st each side on back, and 1 st each side on front.

2) When picking up sts for armbands, pick up sts ½ st from edge on back and 1 st from edge on front.

3) When sewing side seams, seam ½ st from edge on back and 1 st from edge on front.

K2, P2 RIB

(multiple of 4 sts plus 2)

Row 1 (WS) P2, *k2, p2; rep from * to end.

Row 2 K2, *p2, k2; rep from * to end.

Rep rows 1 and 2 for k2, p2 rib.

BACK

With size 17 (12.75mm) needles and MC, cast on 38 (38, 42) sts. Work in k2, p2 rib for 5 rows, end with a WS row. Change to size 19 (15mm) needles.

Next (dec) row (RS) Knit across, dec 7 (5, 5) sts evenly spaced—31 (33, 37) sts. Beg with a purl row, work in St st for 3 (5, 5) rows more, end with a WS row. Cont in St st and stripe pat as foll: [8 (9, 10) rows CC, 8 (9, 10) rows MC] twice, end with a WS row. Piece should measure approx 18½ (21, 23)"/47 (53.5, 58.5)cm from beg.

Shoulder shaping

Cont stripe pat as foll:

Next row (RS) With MC, bind off first 5 (5, 6) sts, cut MC; join B and k21 (23, 25); join MC and bind off last 5 (5, 6) sts, cut MC. With CC, bind off 4 (5, 6) sts at beg of next 2 rows—13 sts. Purl next row. Bind off sts knitwise.

FRONT

With size 15 (10mm) needles and MC, cast on 50 (54, 58) sts. Work in k2, p2 rib for 4"/10cm, end with a WS row.

Next (dec) row (RS) Knit across, dec 2 sts evenly spaced—48 (52, 56) sts. Beg with a purl row, working St st until piece measures 10½ (12½, 14)"/26.5 (32, 35.5)cm from beg, end with a WS row.

Divide for placket opening

Next row (RS) K21 (23, 25), join a 2nd ball of MC and bind off center 6 sts, k to end. Working both sides at once, work even until piece measures 15½ (18, 20)"/39.5 (45.5, 51)cm from beg, end with a WS row.

Neck shaping

Bind off 3 sts from each neck edge once, then 2 sts once, end with a WS row.

Next (dec) row (RS) With first ball of yarn, knit to last 3 sts, k2tog, k1; with 2nd ball of yarn, k1, ssk, knit to end. Purl next row. Rep last 2 rows twice more. Work even on 13 (15, 17) sts each side until piece measures same length as back to shoulder, end with a WS row.

Shoulder shaping

Bind off 5 (5, 6) sts at beg of next 2 rows, 4 (5, 6) sts at beg of next 2 rows, then 4 (5, 5) sts at beg of next 2 rows.

FINISHING

Sew shoulder seams.

Button band

With RS facing, size 17 (12.75mm) needles and

MC, pick up and k 12 sts evenly spaced along left front placket opening.

Row 1 (WS) *P2, k2; rep from * to end. Rep this row 3 times more. Bind off in rib.

Buttonhole band

With RS facing, size 17 (12.75mm) needles and MC, pick up and k 12 sts evenly spaced along right front placket opening.

Row 1 (WS) *K2, p2; rep from * to end.

Row 2 (buttonhole–RS) K2, p2, k2, p1, yo, k2tog, k1, p2.

Rows 3 and 4 Rep row 1. Bind off in rib.

Neckband

With RS facing, size 17 (12.75mm) needles and MC, pick up and k 15 sts evenly spaced along right front neck edge to shoulder seam, 16 sts along back neck edge, then 15 sts along left neck edge—46 sts.

Row 1 (WS) P2, *k2, p2; rep from * to end.

Row 2 (buttonhole–RS) K2, yo, p2tog, k2, *p2, k2; rep from * to end.

Row 3 Rep row 1.

Row 4 K2, *p2, k2; rep from * to end. Bind off in rib. Place markers 8 (8½, 9)"/20.5 (21.5, 23)cm down from shoulders on back and front.

Left armband

With RS facing, size 15 (10mm) needles and MC, pick up and k 21 (22, 23) sts evenly spaced along left front armhole to shoulder seam, then pick up and k 16 (17, 18) sts evenly spaced along left back armhole to marker—37 (39, 41) sts.

Next (inc) row (WS) K0 (0, 2), p1 (2, 1), M1 p-st, p1, k3, M1 p-st, p2, M1, k2, p1, M1 p-st, p1, k3, p1,

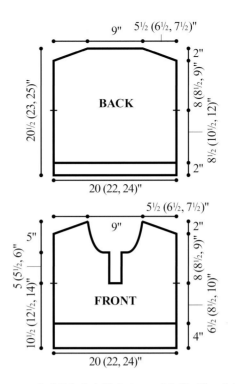

M1 p-st, p1; k3 [p3, k3] 3 times, k0 (1, 0), p0 (0, 2)—42 (44, 46) sts. Cont in rib pat as established for 4 rows more. Bind off in rib, dec 1 st 3 sts before shoulder seam, 1 st at shoulder seam and 1 st 3 sts after shoulder seam.

Right armband

With RS facing, size 15 (10mm) needles and MC, pick up and k 16 (17, 18) sts evenly spaced along right back armhole to shoulder seam, then pick up and k 21 (22, 23) sts evenly spaced along right front armhole to marker—37 (39, 41) sts.

Next (inc) row (WS) P0 (0, 2), k3 (4, 3), [p3, k3] 3 times; p1, M1 p-st, p1, k3, p1, M1 p-st, p1, k2, M1, p2, M1 p-st, k3, p1, M1 p-st, p1 (2, 1), k0 (0, 2)—42 (44, 46) sts. Cont in rib pat as established for 4 rows more. Bind off in rib, dec 1 st 3 sts before shoulder seam, 1 st at shoulder seam and 1 st 3 sts after shoulder seam. Sew side and armband seams. Sew on buttons. ■

Oversized Striped Pullover

Colorway interplay is the name of the game on Maie Landra's welted cowl-neck pullover. She stripes the body by alternating two variegated multi-shade yarns with one solid to harmonious effect.

SIZES

Sized for X-Small, Small, Medium, Large, 1X, 2X, 3X and shown in size Medium.

KNITTED MEASUREMENTS

Bust 35 (39, 43, 47, 51, 55, 59)"/89 (99, 109, 119, 129.5, 139.5, 149.5)cm
Length 25½ (26½, 27, 27½, 28½, 29 29½)"/64.5 (67, 68.5, 69.5, 72.5, 73.5, 75)cm
Upper arm 11 (13, 14½, 16, 16½, 18, 19½)"/28 (33, 37, 40.5, 42, 45.5, 49)cm

MATERIALS

• 3 (3, 4, 4, 5, 5, 6) 1¾oz/50g hanks (each approx 175yd/160m) of Koigu *Painter's Palette Premium Merino* (wool) each in #P470 medium purple multi (A) and #P817X dark purple multi (B) **①**

• 6 (7, 7, 8, 8, 9, 10) 1¾oz/50g hanks (each approx 175yd/160m) of Koigu *Premium Merino* (wool) in #2160 purple solid (C) **①**

• One pair size 4 (3.5mm) needles OR SIZE TO OBTAIN GAUGE

• Size 4 (3.5mm) circular needle, 16"/40cm long

GAUGE

26 sts and 34 rows = 4"/10cm over St st size 4 (3.5mm) needles.
TAKE TIME TO CHECK GAUGE.

RIDGE PATTERN (for back and front)

[3 rows A in rev St st, 3 rows B in rev St st, 4 rows C in St st] 10 times.

RIDGE PATTERN (for sleeves)

[6 rows C in rev St st, 2 rows A in St st, 2 rows B in St st] 10 times.

RIDGE PATTERN (for neckband)

*6 rnds St st with C, 4 rnds rev St st with A, 6 rnds St st with C, 4 rnds rev St st with B; rep from * (20 rnds) for ridge pat for neckband.

STRIPE PATTERN

*3 rows A, 3 rows B, 4 rows C; rep from * (10 rows) for stripe pat.

BACK

With straight needles, cast on 114 (126, 140, 152, 166, 178, 192) sts. Work 100 rows in ridge pat for back. Cont in St st and stripe pat to end of piece, AT SAME TIME, when piece measures 18½ (19, 19, 19, 19½, 19½, 19½)"/47 (48, 48, 48, 49.5, 49.5, 49.5)cm from beg, work as foll:

Armhole shaping

Bind off 3 (4, 5, 6, 6, 7, 7) sts at beg of next 2 rows, 2 (3, 4, 5, 5, 5, 6) sts at beg of next 2 rows, 0 (0, 0, 0, 2, 3, 3) sts at beg of next 0 (0, 0, 0, 4, 6, 8) rows. Dec 1 st each side every other row 3 (6, 6, 8, 9, 8, 9) times—98 (100, 110, 114, 118, 120, 124) sts. Work even until armhole measures 6 (6½, 7, 7½, 8, 8½, 9)"/15 (16.5, 18, 19, 20.5, 21.5, 23)cm.

Neck shaping

Next row (RS) Work 33 (33, 38, 40, 41, 42, 43) sts, join 2nd ball of yarn and bind off center 32 (34, 34, 34, 36, 36, 38) sts, work to end. Working both sides at once, bind off from each neck edge 2 sts twice. Work even until armhole measures 7 (7½, 8, 8½, 9, 9½, 10)"/17.5 (19, 20.5, 21.5, 23, 24, 25.5)cm. Bind off rem 29 (29, 34, 36, 37, 38, 39) sts each side for shoulders.

FRONT

Work as for back until armhole measures 3½ (4, 4½, 5, 5½, 6, 6½)"/9 (10, 11.5, 12.5, 14, 15, 16.5)cm.

Neck shaping

Next row (RS) K35 (35, 40, 42, 43, 44, 45), join 2nd ball of yarn and bind off center 28 (30, 30, 30, 32, 32, 34) sts, work to end. Working both sides at once, bind off from each neck edge 2 sts once, then dec 1 st at each neck edge every other row 4 times.

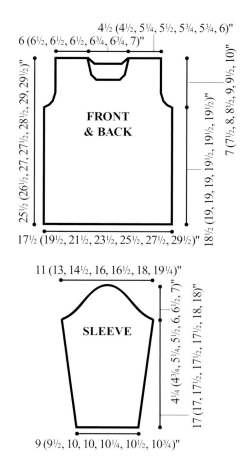

Work even on rem 29 (29, 34, 36, 37, 38, 39) sts each side until armhole measures same length as back. Bind off sts each side for shoulders.

SLEEVES

With straight needles, cast on 58 (62, 64, 64, 66, 68, 70) sts. Work 100 rows in ridge pat for sleeves, then cont in St st and beg with 4 rows C, work in stripe pat to end of sleeve, AT SAME TIME, work 40 (40, 40, 40, 40, 20, 40) rows even, then inc 1 st each side on next row, then every 18th (12th, 8th,

6th, 6th, 6th, 4th) row 6 (10, 14, 19, 20, 23, 27) times more—72 (84, 94, 104, 108, 116, 126) sts. Work even until piece measures 17 (17, 17½, 17½, 17½, 18, 18)"/43 (43, 44.5, 44.5, 44.5, 45.5, 45.5)cm from beg.

Cap shaping

Bind off 3 (4, 5, 6, 6, 7, 7) sts at beg of next 2 rows, 2 (3, 4, 5, 5, 5, 6) sts at beg of next 2 rows, dec 1 st each side every other row 6 (6, 6, 8, 10, 11, 11) times. Bind off 2 sts at beg next 20 (24, 28, 28, 28, 30, 34) rows. Bind off rem 10 sts.

FINISHING

Block pieces to measurements. Sew shoulder seams.

Cowl neckband

With RS facing, circular needle and C, pick up and k 136 sts evenly around neck edge. Work in ridge pat for neckband as foll: Work 25 rnds even. Inc 10 sts evenly spaced on next rnd—146 sts. Work 14 rnds even. Inc 10 sts evenly spaced on next rnd—156 sts. Work 9 rnds even. Inc 10 sts evenly spaced on next rnd—166 sts. Work 9 rnds even. Inc 10 sts evenly spaced on next rnd—176 sts. Work even until 116 rnds in total have been worked in ridge pat. Bind off sts loosely. Set in sleeves. Sew side and sew sleeve seams. ■

Striped Tunic

Faith Hale's oversized striped pullover, knit to tunic length in blue and gray, gets an unexpected pop of color from paprika-hued ribbed cuffs.

SIZES

Sized for Small, Medium, Large, 1X, 2X and shown in size Small.

KNITTED MEASUREMENTS

Bust 44½ (46½, 49, 53, 56)"/113 (118, 124.5, 134.5, 142)cm

Length 31½(32¼, 33½, 34, 34½)"/80 (82, 85, 86, 87.5)cm

Upper arm 16 (17, 18½, 19½, 20½)"/40.5 (43, 46.5, 49.5, 52)cm

MATERIALS

• 7 (8, 9, 9, 10) 1¾oz/50g skeins (each approx 76yd/70m) of Bergère de France *Cocoon* (acrylic/mohair/alpaca) in #241.651 blue (A) 🄵

• 5 (6, 6, 7, 7) skeins in #241.481 dark grey (B)

• 2 (2, 3, 3, 3) skeins in #241.621 red (C)

• One pair size 10½ (6.5mm) needles OR SIZE TO OBTAIN GAUGE

• One set (5) size 10½ (6.5mm) double-pointed needles (dpns)

GAUGE

14 sts and 20 rows = 4"/10cm over St st using size 10½ (6.5mm) needles.
TAKE TIME TO CHECK GAUGE.

BACK

With A, cast on 78 (82, 86, 94, 98) sts.

Row 1 (RS) K2, *p2, k2; rep from * to end.

Cont in k2, p2 rib until piece measures 5"/12.5cm from beg.

Beg stripe pattern

Rows 1-4 With B, work 4 rows in St st.

Rows 5-8 With A, work 4 rows in St st.

Rep these 8 rows for stripe pat until piece measures 17"/43cm from beg.

Place markers each side of last row to mark the beg of armholes. Work even until piece measures 8½ (9, 9½, 10, 10½)"/21.5 (23, 24, 25.5, 26.5)cm from the markers.

Shoulder shaping

Dec row (RS) K2tog, k to last 2 sts, ssk. Rep dec row every other row 10 (11, 13, 13, 13) times more.

Bind off 4 (4, 4, 4, 6) sts at beg of next 8 (8, 8, 2, 2) rows, 5 sts at beg of next 0 (0, 0, 6, 6) rows.

Bind off rem 24 (26, 26, 28, 28) sts.

FRONT

Work as for back until piece measures 6½ (7, 7, 7½, 8)"/16.5 (18, 18, 19, 20.5)cm from markers.

Neck shaping

Next row (RS) K37 (38, 40, 43, 45), join a 2nd ball of yarn and bind off center 4 (6, 6, 8, 8) sts, k to end.

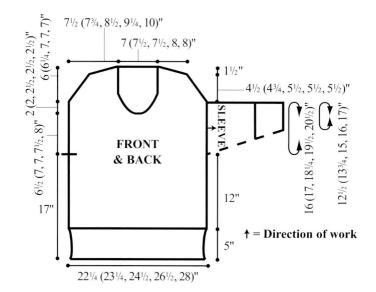

Working both sides at once, bind off 2 sts from each neck edge twice.

Dec row (RS) K to the last 3 sts of first side, k2tog, k1; on 2nd side, k1, ssk, k to end.

Rep dec row every other row 5 times more, AT SAME TIME, when armhole measures 8½ (9, 9½, 10, 10½)"/21.5 (23, 24, 25.5, 26.5)cm from markers, work as foll:

Shoulder shaping

Dec row (RS) K2tog, k to the end of the first side; on 2nd side, k to the last 2 sts, ssk. Rep dec row every other row 10 (11, 13, 13, 13) times more. Then, bind off 4 (4, 4, 4, 6) sts from each shoulder edge 4 (4, 4, 1, 1) times, then 5 sts 0 (0, 0, 3, 3) times.

FINISHING

Block pieces to measurements, omitting ribbing. Sew shoulder seams.

SLEEVES

With dpns and B, pick up and k 56 (60, 64, 68, 72) sts evenly between markers. Divide sts evenly onto 4 dpns with 14 (15, 16, 17, 18) sts on each needle. Join, being careful not to twist sts, and pm to mark beg of rnds. Work in rnds of St st (k every rnd) working stripe pat of 4 rnds B, 4 rnds A as before, AT SAME TIME, after 7 rnds are worked, work as foll:

Dec rnd K2tog, k to the last 2 sts, ssk. Rep dec rnd every 4th rnd 5 times more—44 (48, 52, 56, 60) sts. Work even with A for 4 rnds more. Then, change to C and work as foll:

Next rnd Knit.

Next rnd * K2, p2; rep from * around. Cont in rnds of k2, p2 rib for a total of 5"/12.5cm. Bind off in rib. Sew side seams.

Neckband

With dpns and A, pick up and k 80 (84, 84, 88, 88) sts evenly around neck. Join and pm to mark beg of rnds. Work in rnds of k2, p2 rib for 4 rnds. Bind off in rib. ■

Cropped Seed Stitch Pullover

Exaggerated two-row stripes of seed stitching and long sleeves juxtapose the cropped length of Annabelle Speer's pullover, worked in beguiling shades of brick and copper.

SIZES

Sized for Small, Medium, Large, X-Large and shown in size Small.

KNITTED MEASUREMENTS

Bust 36 (40, 44, 48)"/91.5 (101.5, 111.5, 122)cm
Length 15½ (16½, 17, 18)"/39.5 (42, 43, 45.5)cm
Upper arm 14½ (14½, 15, 15¾)"/37 (37, 38, 40)cm

MATERIALS

• 3 (3, 4, 4) 3½oz/100g hanks (each approx 137yd/125m) of Manos del Uruguay/Fairmount Fibers *Wool Clasica* (wool) each in #54 brick (A) and #28 copper (B) **④**

• One pair size 8 (5mm) needles OR SIZE TO OBTAIN GAUGE

• Size 8 (5mm) circular needle, 16"/40cm long

• 2 stitch holders and stitch marker

GAUGE

13 sts and 24 rows = 4"/10cm over St st using size 8 (5mm) needles.
TAKE TIME TO CHECK GAUGE.

SEED STITCH

(over an odd number of sts)
Row 1 (RS) K1, *p1, k1; rep from * to end.
Row 2 P the knit sts and k the purl sts.
Rep row 2 for seed st.

BACK

With straight needles and A, cast on 59 (65, 71, 79) sts. Work 1 row in seed st. Cont in seed st, work 2 rows more in A, 2 rows in B. Rep last 4 rows for seed st stripe pat until piece measures 8½ (9, 9, 9½)"/21.5 (23, 23, 24)cm from beg, end with a WS row.

Armhole shaping

Bind off 3 (3, 4, 5) sts at beg of next 2 rows.
Next (dec) row (RS) K2tog tbl, work in pat to last 2 sts, k2tog. Rep dec row every other row 2 (3, 3, 5)

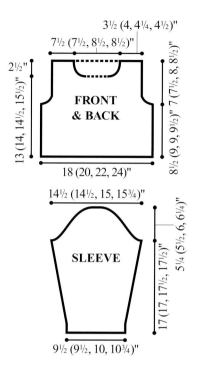

3½ (4, 4¼, 4½)"

7½ (7½, 8½, 8½)"

2½"

13 (14, 14½, 15½)"

8½ (9, 9½, 10½)"

7 (7½, 8, 8½)"

FRONT
& BACK

18 (20, 22, 24)"

14½ (14½, 15, 15¾)"

SLEEVE

17 (17, 17½, 17½)"

5¼ (5½, 6, 6¼)"

9½ (9½, 10, 10¾)"

times more—47 (51, 55, 57) sts. Work even in pat until armhole measures 7 (7½, 8, 8½)"/18 (19, 20.5, 21.5)cm. Bind off 11 (13, 14, 15) sts at beg of next 2 rows, place rem 25 (25, 27, 27) sts on a stitch holder for back neck.

FRONT

Work as for back until armhole measures 4½ (5, 5½, 6)"/11.5 (12.5, 14, 15)cm, end with a WS row.

Neck shaping

Next row (RS) Work 18 (20, 22, 23) sts, place next 11 sts on a stitch holder, join a 2nd ball of yarn and work to end of row. Working both sides at once, bind off 2 sts from each neck edge twice, then dec 1 st every other row 3 (3, 4, 4) times— 11 (13, 14, 15) sts rem each side. Work even in pat until piece measures same as back to shoulder. Bind off.

SLEEVES

With straight needles and A, cast on 31 (31, 33, 35) sts. Work one row in seed st. Cont in seed st stripe pat as for back until 8 rows are complete.

Next row (RS) Inc 1 st at each side, working inc'd sts into pat. Cont in pat as established and rep inc row every 10th row 3 times more, then every 14th row 4 times—47 (47, 49, 51) sts. Work even until piece measures 17 (17, 17½, 17½)"/43 (43, 44.5, 44.5)cm from beg, end with a WS row.

Cap shaping

Bind off 3 (3, 4, 5) sts at beg of next 2 rows, then dec 1 st at each side of every other row 14 (14, 15, 15) times. Work 0 (2, 2, 4) rows even. Bind off 4 (4, 3, 3) sts at beg of next 2 rows, bind off rem 5 sts.

FINISHING

Block pieces lightly to measurements. Sew shoulder seams.

Collar

With RS facing, circular needle and A, beg at left shoulder seam and pick up and k 12 sts along left front neck edge, k11 from front neck holder, pick up and k 12 sts along right front neck edge, k25 (25, 27, 27) from back neck holder—60 (60, 62, 62) sts. Join and place marker for beg of rnd.
Rnd 1 *K1, p1; rep from * to end.
Rnd 2 *P1, k1; rep from * to end.
Rep rnd 1 once more, then bind off loosely in pat. Set in sleeves. Sew side and sleeve seams. ■

Striped Turtleneck

The red and brown colorways and flattering waist shaping update the look of Kaffe Fassett's classic turtleneck worked in stockinette stripes with ribbing at the hemline, cuffs, and collar.

SIZES

Sized for Small, Medium, Large, 1X, 2X and shown in size Small.

KNITTED MEASUREMENTS

Bust 34 (38, 42, 46, 50)"/86.5 (96.5, 106.5, 117, 127)cm

Length 22½ (23, 24½, 26, 26½)"/57 (58.5, 62, 66, 67.5)cm

Upper arm 13 (14, 15, 16, 17)"/ 33 (35.5, 38, 40.5, 43)cm

MATERIALS

• 2 (2, 3, 3, 4) 3½oz/100g balls (each approx 462yd/420m) of Schachenmayr Regia/Westminster Fibers *Regia Design Line Hand-Dye Effect by Kaffe Fassett* (wool/polyamide/acrylic) each in #86883 brown (A) and #86888 red (B) (**1**)

• One pair each sizes 1 and 2 (2.5 and 2.75mm) needles OR SIZE TO OBTAIN GAUGE

GAUGE

30 sts and 40 rows = 4"/10cm over St st using larger needles.
TAKE TIME TO CHECK GAUGE.

K1, P1 RIB

(multiple of 2 sts plus 1)

Row 1 (RS) K1, *p1, k1; rep from * to end.

Row 2 P1, *k1, p1; rep from * to end.

Rep rows 1 and 2 for k1, p1 rib.

STRIPE PATTERN

Working in St st, *work 4 rows A, 4 rows B; rep from * (8 rows) for stripe pat.

BACK

With smaller needles and A, cast on 127 (143, 157, 173, 187) sts. Work in k1, p1 rib for 20 rows, AT SAME TIME, work in stripe pat. Change to larger needles and St st. Cont in stripe pat as established and work even until piece measures 2½ (2½, 3, 3½, 3½)"/6.5 (6.5, 7.5, 9, 9)cm from beg, end with a WS row.

Waist shaping

Dec 1 st each side on next row, then every 6th row 6 times more—113 (129, 143, 159, 173) sts. Work even until piece measures 8 (8, 8½, 9, 9)"/20.5 (20.5, 21.5, 23, 23)cm from beg, end with a WS row. Inc 1 st each side on next row, then every 6th row 6 times more—127 (143, 157, 173, 187) sts. Work even until piece measures approx 14 (14, 15, 16 16)"/35.5 (35.5, 38, 40.5, 40.5)cm from beg, end with 4 rows A (A, B, B, B).

Armhole shaping

Bind off 6 (7, 8, 9, 10) sts at beg of next 2 rows, then 3 (4, 4, 5, 6) sts at beg of next 2 rows. Dec 1 st each side on next row, then every other row 5 (7, 9, 11, 13) times more—97 (105, 113, 121, 127) sts. Work even until armhole measures 7½ (8, 8½, 9, 9½)"/19 (20.5, 21.5, 23, 24)cm, end with a WS row.

Shoulder shaping

Bind off 6 (7, 8, 9, 9) sts at beg of next 4 rows, then 7 (8, 8, 9, 10) sts at beg of next 4 rows. Bind off rem 45 (45, 49, 49, 51) sts for back neck.

FRONT

Work as for back until armhole measures 5 (5½, 6, 6½, 7)"/12.5 (14, 15, 16.5, 17.5)cm, end with a WS row.

Neck shaping

Next row (RS) K39 (43, 45, 49, 51), join a 2nd ball of yarn and bind off center 19 (19, 23, 23, 25) sts, knit to end. Working both sides at once, bind off 3 sts from each neck edge once, then 2 sts twice, end with a WS row. Dec 1 st from each neck edge on next row, then every other row 5 times more. Work even on rem 26 (30, 32, 36, 38) sts each side until piece measures same length as back to shoulder, end with a WS row. Shape shoulders as for back.

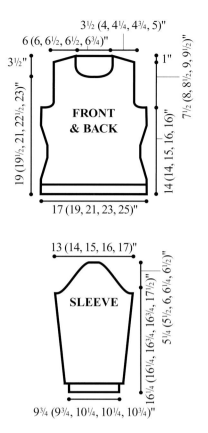

3½ (4, 4¼, 4¾, 5)"
6 (6, 6½, 6½, 6¾)"
3½"
19 (19½, 21, 22½, 23)"
FRONT & BACK
14 (14, 15, 16, 16)"
7½ (8, 8½, 9, 9½)"
1"
17 (19, 21, 23, 25)"

13 (14, 15, 16, 17)"
SLEEVE
16¼ (16¼, 16¾, 16¾, 17½)"
5¼ (5½, 6, 6¼, 6½)"
9¾ (9¾, 10¼, 10¼, 10¾)"

SLEEVES

With smaller needles and A, cast on 73 (73, 77, 77, 81) sts. Work in k1, p1 rib for 20 rows, AT SAME TIME, work in stripe pat. Change to larger needles and St st. Cont in stripe pat as established and work 8 rows even. Inc 1 st each side on next row, then every 6th row 0 (0, 3, 15, 22) times more, every 8th row 0 (12, 14, 5, 0) times, every 10th row 3 (3, 0, 0, 0) times, then every 12th row 8 (0, 0, 0, 0) times—97 (105, 113, 119, 127) sts. Work even until piece measures approx 16¼ (16¼, 16¾, 17½, 17½)"/41 (41, 42.5, 44.5, 44.5)cm from beg, end with 4 rows A (A, B, B, B).

Cap shaping

Bind off 6 (7, 8, 9, 10) sts at beg of next 2 rows, then 3 (4, 4, 5, 6) sts at beg of next 2 rows. Dec 1 st each side on next row, then every other row 20 (22, 24, 25, 27) times more. Bind off 4 sts at beg of next 6 rows. Bind off rem 13 (13, 15, 15, 15) sts.

FINISHING

Block pieces to measurements. Sew shoulder seams.

TURTLENECK

With larger needles and A, cast on 157 (157, 169, 169, 175) sts. Change to smaller needles. Work in k1, p1 rib and stripe pat until piece measures approx 8 (8, 8½, 8½, 9)"/20.5 (20.5, 21.5, 21.5, 23)cm from beg, end with a completed stripe. With larger needle, bind off loosely in rib. Using mattress stitch, sew side edges of turtleneck tog, matching stripes. Placing seam at center back neck edge, pin bound-off edge of turtleneck to neck edge, so WS of turtleneck is facing RS of sweater. Sew turtleneck in place. Set in sleeves, matching stripes. Sew side and sleeve seams, matching stripes. ■

Heart Yoke Pullover

The yoke of this pullover by Ruth Garcia-Alcantud is stitched in a Fair Isle hearts-and-diamonds pattern. The wide-necked sweater is worked in the round from the corrugated rib up for a new take on an old technique.

SIZES

Sized for X-Small, Small, Medium, Large and shown in size X-Small.

KNITTED MEASUREMENTS

Bust 31 (33, 35, 37)"/78.5 (83.5, 89, 94)cm
Length 21½ (22½, 23¼, 24)"/54.5 (57, 59, 61)cm
Upper arm 10 (11, 12, 13)"/25.5 (28, 30.5, 33)cm

MATERIALS

• 5 (6, 7, 7) 1¾oz/50g skeins (each approx 184yd/168m) of Brown Sheep *Nature Spun Sport* (wool) in #880 charcoal (A) 🔳

• 1 skein each of #601 pepper (B) and #N03 gray heather (C)

• One each size 5 (3.75mm) circular needle, 16"/40cm and 32"/80cm long, OR SIZE TO OBTAIN GAUGE

• One set (5) size 5 (3.75) double-pointed needles (dpns)

• Stitch markers and stitch holder

GAUGES

24 sts and 32 rnds = 4"/10cm over St st using size 5 (3.75mm) needle.
24 sts and 28 rnds = 4"/10cm over St st and yoke chart pat using size 5 (3.75mm) needle.
TAKE TIME TO CHECK GAUGES.

NOTE

Body of pullover and sleeves are worked in the round. A purl st is worked at each side, creating a "faux seam."

BODY

With B and longer circular needle, cast on 188 (200, 212, 224) sts. Join to work in rnds, being careful not to twist sts, and pm to mark beg of rnds.

Two-color rib

Rnd 1 *With A, k2, with B, p2; rep from * around.
Rep rnd 1 for two-color rib until piece measures 1"/2.5cm from beg. Then, cont with A only, work as foll:
Next rnd With A, *p1, k93 (99, 105, 111); rep from * once more. Rep the last rnd (with the p1 "faux seam" as established) until piece measures 2"/5cm from beg.

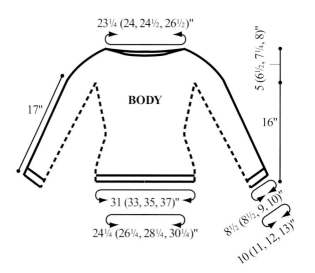

BODY

23¼ (24, 24½, 26½)"

5 (6½, 7¼, 8)"

17"

16"

31 (33, 35, 37)"

24¼ (26¼, 28¼, 30¼)"

8½ (8½, 9, 10)"

10 (11, 12, 13)"

Dec rnd *P1, k2, SKP, k to 4 sts before the p1 "faux seam," k2tog, k2; rep from * once more—4 sts dec'd.

Rep dec rnd every 4th rnd 7 times more, then every 2nd rnd twice—148 (160, 172, 184) sts. Work even until piece measures 8"/20.5cm from beg.

Inc rnd *P1, k1, kfb in next st, k to 2 sts before the p1 "faux seam," kfb, k1; rep from * once more—4 sts inc'd.

Rep inc rnd every 4th rnd 8 times more, then every 6th rnd once—188 (200, 212, 224) sts. Work even until piece measures 16"/40.5cm from beg, AT SAME TIME, on the last rnd worked, place a marker in the 141st (150th, 159th, 168th) st from beg to indicate the center back.

Armhole shaping

Next rnd K9 and sl these sts to a st holder (for armhole), k77 (83, 89, 95); then k17 and sl these last sts to a st holder (for armhole), k77 (83, 89, 95), sl the last 8 sts to a st holder (for armhole). Cut yarn and set piece aside.

SLEEVES

With dpns and B, cast on 52 (52, 56, 60) sts. Join to work in rib, being careful not to twist sts, and pm to mark beg of rnds. Work in two-color rib as on body for 1¼"/3cm. Then cont with A only, work as foll:

Next rnd With A, p1, k51 (51, 55, 59).

Rep the last rnd for 21 (11, 11, 11) rnds more.

Inc rnd *P1, k1, kfb in next st, k to the last 2 sts, kfb, k1. Rep inc rnd every 22nd (12th, 12th, 12th) rnd 3 (6, 7, 8) times more—60 (66, 72, 78) sts. Work even until piece measures 17"/43cm from beg.

Cap Shaping

Next rnd K9 and sl these sts to a st holder, k43 (49, 55, 61), k8 and sl these sts to st holder. Cut yarn and set piece aside. Work 2nd sleeve.

YOKE

Rejoin A to the marked st on the body (the marker indicating the center back).

Rnd 1 With A, k to back armhole, pm; k 43 (49, 55, 61) sts from first sleeve, pm; k 77 (83, 89, 95) sts of front, pm; k 43 (49, 55, 61) sts of 2nd sleeve, pm; k rem sts of back, pm to mark beg of rnd—240 (264, 288, 312) sts.

For sizes (Small, Medium, Large) only

Dec rnd 1 *K to 3 sts before marker, k2tog, k1, sl marker, k1, SKP; rep from * 3 times more, k to end of rnd—8 sts dec'd.

Work even for 3 rnds more.

Rep the last 4 rows (0, 1, 2) times more—(256, 272, 288) sts.

For size Small only

Dec rnd 2 *K to 3 sts before marker, k2tog, k1, sl marker; work even across sleeve sts, sl marker, k1, SKP, k to 3 sts before marker, k2tog, k1, work even across sleeve sts, sl marker, k1, SKP, k to end—4 sts dec'd for 252 sts.

For size Medium only

Dec rnd Rep dec rnd 1—8 sts dec'd for 264 sts.

For all sizes

There are 240 (252, 264, 288) sts at this point.

Beg yoke pat chart

Rnd 2 Beg with rnd 2 of chart, join C and work the 12-st rep for 20 (21, 22, 24) reps. Cont to foll chart through rnd 29. After completing chart, there are 200 (210, 220, 240) sts. Cut B.

Next dec rnd [S2KP, k7] 20 (21, 22, 24) times—160 (168, 176, 192) sts.

Work 0 (2, 4, 6) rnds even.

Next dec rnd [K6, ssk] 20 (21, 22, 24) times—140 (147, 154, 168) sts.

For sizes (Small, Medium, Large) only

Next dec rnd Knit, dec'ing (3, 6, 8) sts evenly spaced—(144, 148, 160) sts.

For all sizes

Join B and work in two-color rib for 5 rnds. Bind off in rib with B.

FINISHING

Graft the matching underarm sts tog from holders. Block finished piece lightly to measurements. ■

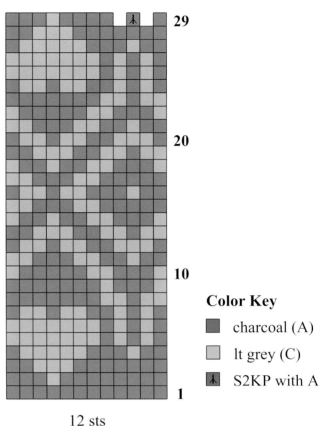

29

20

10

1

12 sts

Color Key

■ charcoal (A)

□ lt grey (C)

⅄ S2KP with A

Helpful Information

Abbreviations

approx	approximately
beg	begin(ning)
CC	contrasting color
ch	chain
cm	centimeter(s)
cn	cable needle
cont	continu(e)(ing)
dc	double crochet
dec	decreas(e)(ing)
dpn	double-pointed needle(s)
foll	follow(s)(ing)
g	gram(s)
inc	increas(e)(ing)
k	knit
k2tog	knit 2 sts tog (one st has been decreased)
LH	left-hand
lp(s)	loop(s)
m	meter(s)
M1	make 1 (knit st) by inserting tip of LH needle from front to back under the strand between the last stitch and the next stitch; knit into the back loop
M1 p-st	make 1 purl st
MC	main color
mm	millimeter(s)
oz	ounce(s)
p	purl
p2tog	purl 2 stitches together
pat(s)	pattern(s)
pm	place marker
psso	pass slip stitch(es) over
rem	remain(s)(ing)
rep	repeat
RH	right-hand
rnd(s)	round(s)
RS	right side(s)
S2KP	slip 2 sts tog, knit 1, pass 2 slip sts over knit 1 (two sts have been decreased)
sc	single crochet
SKP	slip 1, knit 1, pass slip st over (one st has been decreased)
SK2P	slip 1, knit 2 tog, pass slip st over the knit 2 tog (two sts have been decreased)
sl	slip
sl st	slip stitch
ssk (ssp)	slip next 2 stitches knitwise (purlwise), one at a time; knit (purl) these 2 stitches tog
sssk	slip next 3 stitches knitwise, one at a time; knit these 3 stitches together
st(s)	stitch(es)
St st	stockinette stitch
tbl	through back loop(s)
tog	together
tr	treble crochet
WS	wrong side(s)
wyib	with yarn in back
wyif	with yarn in front
yd	yard(s)
yo	yarn over needle
*	repeat directions following*
[ ]	repeat directions inside brackets as many times as indicated

Knitting Needles

U.S.	METRIC
0	2mm
1	2.25mm
2	2.75mm
3	3.25mm
4	3.5mm
5	3.75mm
6	4mm
7	4.5mm
8	5mm
9	5.5mm
10	6mm
10½	6.5mm
11	8mm
13	9mm
15	10mm
17	12.75mm
19	15mm
35	19mm

Skill Levels

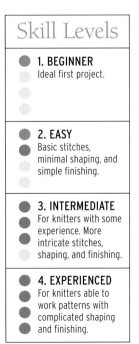

1. BEGINNER
Ideal first project.

2. EASY
Basic stitches, minimal shaping, and simple finishing.

3. INTERMEDIATE
For knitters with some experience. More intricate stitches, shaping, and finishing.

4. EXPERIENCED
For knitters able to work patterns with complicated shaping and finishing.

Resources

ALCHEMY YARNS OF TRANSFORMATION
P.O. Box 1080
Sebastopol, CA 95473
http://www.alchemyyarns.com

ASLAN TRENDS
8 Maple Street
Port Washington, NY 11050
http://www.aslantrends.com

BE SWEET
1315 Bridgeway
Sausalito, CA 94965
www.besweetproducts.com

BERGÈRE DE FRANCE NORTH AMERICA
100 Blvd Marie Victorin
Boucherville, QC J4B 1V6
Canada
www.bergeredefrance.com

BERROCO, INC.
1 Tupperware Drive, Suite 4
North Smithfield, RI 02896-6815
www.berroco.com

BLUE SKY ALPACAS
P.O. Box 387
St. Francis, MN 55070
www.blueskyalpacas.com

BROWN SHEEP COMPANY
100662 County Road 16
Mitchell, Nebraska 69357
www.brownsheep.com

CLASSIC ELITE YARNS
122 Western Avenue
Lowell, MA 01851
www.classiceliteyarns.com

DEBBIE BLISS
Distributed by KFI

FAIRMONT FIBERS LTD.
P. O. Box 2082
Philadelphia, PA 19103
blog.fairmountfibers.com/

HIKOO
Distributed by Skacel Collection, Inc.

Resources, *continued*

KFI
P.O. Box 336
315 Bayview Avenue
Amityville, NY 11701
www.knittingfever.com

KOIGU WOOL DESIGNS
P. O. Box 158
Chatsworth, OH N0h 1G0
Canada
www.koigu.com

KOLLÁGE YARNS
3591 Cahaba Beach Road
Birmingham, AL 35242
www.kollageyarns.com

LION BRAND YARN CO.
34 West 15th Street
New York, NY 10011
www.lionbrand.com

LOUISA HARDING
Distributed by KFI

MANOS DEL URUGUAY
Distributed by Fairmont
Fibers Ltd.
www.manos.com.uy

PLYMOUTH YARN CO.
P.O. Box 28
Bristol, PA 19007
www.plymouthyarn.com

PRISM YARNS
www.prismyarn.com

S. CHARLES COLLEZIONE
Distributed by
Tahki•Stacy Charles, Inc.

SCHULANA
Distributed by Skacel
Collection, Inc.

SKACEL COLLECTION, INC.
http://www.skacelknitting.com

SMC SELECT
Distributed by
Westminster Fibers

TAHKI YARNS
Distributed by
Tahki•Stacy Charles, Inc.

TAHKI•STACY CHARLES, INC.
70-30 80th Street, Building 36
Ridgewood, NY 11385
www.tahkistacycharles.com

TRENDSETTER YARNS
16745 Saticoy Street, Suite 101
Van Nuys, CA 91406
www.trendsetteryarns.com

ZITRON
Distributed by Skacel Collection, Inc.

WESTMINSTER FIBERS
165 Ledge Street
Nashua, NH 03060
www.westminsterfibers.com

Yarn Substitutions

The yarns for some of the patterns originally published in *Vogue Knitting* have been discontinued. These are the original yarns:

COWL NECK PULLOVER
(page 34)
5 (6, 6, 7, 7) .88oz/25g balls (each approx 96yd/88m) of Schulana/Skacel Collection *Cashmere Fino* (cashmere) in #08 black (CC)

SWING JACKET (page 53)
16 (18, 19, 20) 1¾ozoz/50g balls (each approx 72yd/70m) of Reynolds/JCA *Garden Tweed* (cotton/linen/ viscose/nylon) in #1 pink tweed

BOAT NECK TOP (page 61)
4 (5, 6, 7, 8, 9) 1¾ozoz/50g hanks each approx 87yd/80m) of Classic Elite Yarns *Four Seasons* (cotton/wool) in #7602 yellow daisy

WAIST TIE TUNIC (page 72)
7 (7, 8, 9, 9) 1¾oz/50g balls (each approx 120yd/110m) of Classic Elite Yarns *Portland Tweed* (wool/rayon/alpaca) in #5058 ruby red (A)

TIE TUNIC (page 96)
14 (16, 17, 18, 19) 1¾oz/50g balls (each approx 81yd/75m) Tahki Yarns/Tahki•Stacy Charles, Inc. *Tweedy Alpaca* (wool/alpaca/acrylic/viscose) in #12 grey

COLLARED CARDI (page 103)
6 (7, 8) 1¾oz/50g balls (each approx 104yd/95m) of Trendsetter Yarns *Vigna* (wool/acrylic) in #478 tiger's eye (B)

CROPPED RAGLAN PULLOVER
(page 104)
11 (12, 14, 16) 1¾oz/50g hanks (each approx 77yd/71m) of Berroco *Bonsai* (bamboo/nylon) in #4103 bamboo

SHAWL COLLAR CARDI
(page 118)
18 (20, 22, 25, 27) 1¾ozoz/50g balls (each approx 87yd/78m) of Classic Elite Yarns *Ariosa* (wool) in #4820 milkweed

CABLED PONCHO (page 140)
12 (15) 1¾ozoz/50g balls (each approx 127yd/117m) of Berroco Blackstone *Tweed Metallic* (wool/ mohair/ angora/other fibers) in #4601 clover honey

RAGLAN TEE (page 163)
2 (2, 2, 3, 3, 4) 4oz/113g hanks (each approx 216yd/198m) of Prism *Rapport* (bamboo/cotton) each in #204 orange (MC) and #305 yellow (CC)

STRIPED BACK TOP (page 165)
4 (5, 6) 7oz/200g hanks (each approx 83yd/76m) of Twinkle Handknits/Classic Elite Yarns *Soft Chunky* (wool) in #51 hazel gray (MC)
1 (1, 1) hanks in #55 midnight (CC)

Standard Yarn Weight System

Categories of yarn, gauge ranges, and recommended needle and hook sizes

Yarn Weight Symbol & Category Names	0 Lace	1 Super Fine	2 Fine	3 Light	4 Medium	5 Bulky	6 Super Bulky
Type of Yarns in Category	Fingering 10 count crochet thread	Sock, Fingering, Baby	Sport, Baby	DK, Light Worsted	Worsted, Afghan, Aran	Chunky, Craft, Rug	Bulky, Roving
Knit Gauge Range* in Stockinette Stitch to 4 inches	33–40** sts	27–32 sts	23–26 sts	21–24 sts	16–20 sts	12–15 sts	6–11 sts
Recommended Needle in Metric Size Range	1.5–2.25 mm	2.25–3.25 mm	3.25–3.75 mm	3.75–4.5 mm	4.5–5.5 mm	5.5–8 mm	8 mm and larger
Recommended Needle U.S. Size Range	000 to 1	1 to 3	3 to 5	5 to 7	7 to 9	9 to 11	11 and larger
Crochet Gauge* Ranges in Single Crochet to 4 inch	32–42 double crochets**	21–32 sts	16–20 sts	12–17 sts	11–14 sts	8–11 sts	5–9 sts
Recommended Hook in Metric Size Range	Steel*** 1.6–1.4mm Regular hook 2.25 mm	2.25–3.5 mm	3.5–4.5 mm	4.5–5.5 mm	5.5–6.5 mm	6.5–9 mm	9 mm and larger
Recommended Hook U.S. Size Range	Steel*** 6, 7, 8 Regular hook B–1	B/1 to E/4	E/4 to 7	7 to I/9	I/9 to K/10½	K/10½ to M/13	M/13 and larger

* GUIDELINES ONLY: The above reflect the most commonly used gauges and needle or hook sizes for specific yarn categories.

** Lace weight yarns are usually knitted or crocheted on larger needles and hooks to create lacy, openwork patterns. Accordingly, a gauge range is difficult to determine. Always follow the gauge stated in your pattern.

*** Steel crochet hooks are sized differently from regular hooks--the higher the number, the smaller the hook, which is the reverse of regular hook sizing.

This Standards & Guidelines booklet and downloadable symbol artwork are available at: **YarnStandards.com**

Useful Techniques

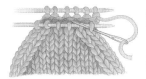

• Kitchener Stitch
1. Insert tapestry needle purlwise (as shown) through first stitch on front needle. Pull yarn through, leaving that stitch on knitting needle.

2. Insert tapestry needle knitwise (as shown) through first stitch on back needle. Pull yarn through, leaving stitch on knitting needle.

3. Insert tapestry needle knitwise through first stitch on front needle, slip stitch off needle and insert tapestry needle purlwise (as shown) through next stitch on front needle. Pull yarn through, leaving this stitch on needle.

4. Insert tapestry needle purlwise through first stitch on back needle. Slip stitch off needle and insert tapestry needle knitwise (as shown) through next stitch on back needle. Pull yarn through, leaving this stitch on needle. Repeat steps 3 and 4 until all stitches on both front and back needles have been grafted. Fasten off and weave in end.

• 3-Needle Bind-Off
1. Hold right sides of pieces together on two needles. Insert third needle knitwise into first st of each needle, and wrap yarn knitwise.

2. Knit these two sts together, and slip them off the needles. *Knit the next two sts together in the same manner.

3. Slip first st on 3rd needle over 2nd st and off needle. Rep from * in step 2 across row until all sts are bound off.

CROCHET STITCHES

• Chain
1. Pass the yarn over the hook and catch it with the hook.

2. Draw the yarn through the loop on the hook.

3. Repeat steps 1 and 2 to make a chain.

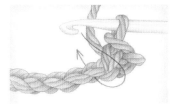

• Single Crochet
1. Insert the hook through top two loops of a stitch. Pass the yarn over the hook and draw up a loop–two loops on hook.

2. Pass the yarn over the hook and draw through both loops on hook.

3. Continue in the same way, inserting the hook into each stitch.

Index

152

180

155

67

108

147

165

76

42

126